Unit C

Move It!
Build It!

Forces and Motion

I WONDER

Wondering is an important part of science. What do you wonder about when you see structures like the ones shown?

Work with a partner to make a list of questions you may have about the forces involved in moving objects to build bridges and other structures. Be ready to share your list with the rest of the class.

◀ **Brooklyn Bridge in New York City**
▼ **Eiffel Tower in Paris, France**

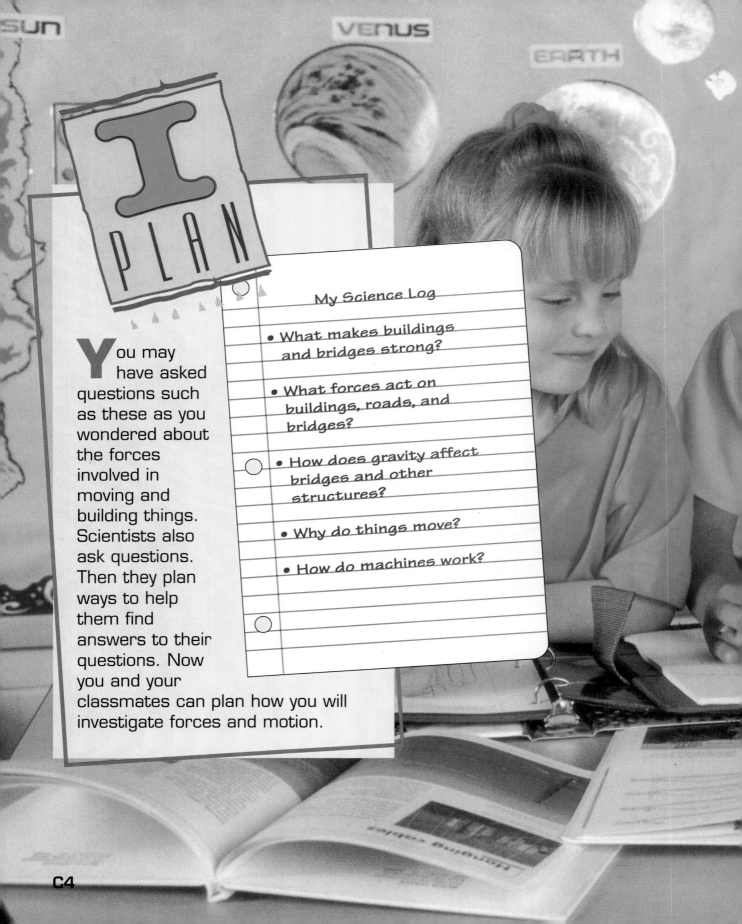

I PLAN

You may have asked questions such as these as you wondered about the forces involved in moving and building things. Scientists also ask questions. Then they plan ways to help them find answers to their questions. Now you and your classmates can plan how you will investigate forces and motion.

My Science Log

- What makes buildings and bridges strong?

- What forces act on buildings, roads, and bridges?

- How does gravity affect bridges and other structures?

- Why do things move?

- How do machines work?

With Your Class

Plan how your class will use the activities and readings from the **I Investigate** part of this unit.

On Your Own

There are many ways to learn about the forces involved in moving and building things. Following are some things you can do to explore forces and motion by yourself or with classmates. Some explorations may take longer to do than others. Look over the suggestions and choose . . .

- **Places to Visit**
- **Projects to Do**
- **Books to Read**

PLACES TO VISIT

CONSTRUCTION SITE

Go with an adult to observe a construction site. Stand a safe distance away. Take notes about or draw pictures of the structure being built. Notice the machines being used. Report to your class about the construction project. If you can, visit the site several times and report on the progress of the project.

BRIDGE

With an adult, visit a bridge in your area. Study how the bridge is made, and find out as much information about it as you can. What does the bridge connect? What does it go over? What type of bridge is it? Take notes about how people use the bridge now. Draw a picture or make a model of the bridge. Show your drawing or model of the bridge to your class as part of a report about the bridge.

SHOPPING CENTER

Visit a shopping center with an adult. Find examples of simple machines—levers, inclined planes, pulleys, wheels and axles. Take a photograph or draw a picture of each simple machine in use. Write down where you saw it. Try to find at least five examples. Make a booklet with your examples, and share it with your class.

PROJECTS TO DO

SCIENCE FAIR PROJECT

Make a bridge, a building, or some other kind of structure out of straws. Use what you learn in this unit to design your structure. See how tall or long or strong you can make it. Draw a picture of your structure and write directions so that someone else can make a structure just like yours. Display your structure and the plans.

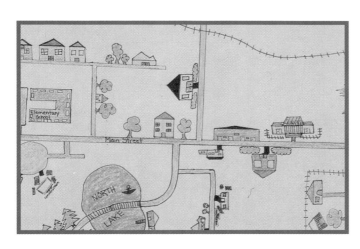

MAPPING

Make a map of your town or community. Mark the locations of interesting buildings, bridges, and other structures. Then mark the locations of current construction sites. Present your map to the class, along with any other interesting information you can find about the structures in your town.

MAKE A MOBILE

Draw pictures of as many examples of simple machines as you can think of. Attach your pictures to a wire coat hanger with thread. Balance them by moving the thread to different places along the hanger. Hang your mobile somewhere in the classroom for others to see.

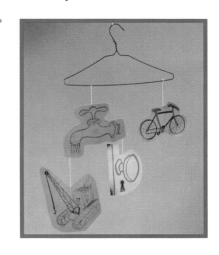

BOOKS TO READ

Galimoto

by Karen Lynn Williams (William Morrow, 1990). A
galimoto is a wonderful toy. If you want one, you must
make it yourself. It is a toy made by children in Africa. It is
made of wires, sticks, or even cornstalks or yams. The toy is
shaped into cars, trucks, bicycles, trains, or helicopters.
Kondi is a boy who wants to make a *galimoto* out of wire.
His big brother is sure he cannot find enough wire to do so.
Read to find out whether Kondi is successful or not.

KAREN LYNN WILLIAMS

GALIMOTO

MULBERRY BOOKS

ILLUSTRATED BY
CATHERINE STOCK

READING RAINBOW Book

Bridges

by Ken Robbins (Dial Books, 1991), Outstanding Science Trade Book. A bridge must be long enough and strong enough to get you safely across it. It can be a simple log across a stream, or it can be a complicated structure of concrete and steel across a river. The pictures in this book show you many kinds of bridges in many different places.

Ken Robbins / Bridges

More Books to Read

Snowshoe Thompson

by Nancy S. Levinson (HarperCollins, 1992), Notable Social Studies Trade Book. Danny's father is in Nevada digging for gold. Danny and his father are separated by snow-covered mountains. How can mail get over the mountains that separate them? This is the story of a real-life pioneer, John Thompson.

The Science Book of Machines

by Neil Ardley (Harcourt Brace, 1992). You use machines every day. From scissors to trains, machines make work seem easier. This book shows you how machines make our lives more convenient.

Balancing

by Terry Jennings (Gloucester Press, 1989). If you can stand on one leg, you are balancing—until you fall over! This book tells you how things balance and how scales work.

Wheels

by Julie Fitzpatrick (Silver Burdett, 1986). Bicycles have them. Skateboards have them. Cars and many other machines have them. Sometimes they turn themselves, and sometimes they make other things turn. They are wheels. Look around and you will see them everywhere. You will learn about them in this book.

INVESTIGATE

To find answers to their questions, scientists read, think, talk to others, and do experiments. In this unit, you will have many chances to think and work like a scientist. How will you find answers to questions you asked?

▶ PREDICTING A prediction is a statement about what you think will happen. To make a prediction, think about what you observed before. Also think about how to interpret the data.

▶ INFERRING Inferring is using what you have observed to explain what has happened. An observation is something you see or experience. An inference is an explanation of your observation, and it may be right or wrong.

▶ FORMULATING AND USING MODELS Objects or events are often too large, too small, or too far away to observe directly. But you can make a model of an object or event and use it to learn more about the real thing.

▶ EXPERIMENTING You experiment to test hypotheses. In a test, you must control variables and gather accurate data. You also must interpret the data and draw conclusions.

Are you ready to begin?

SECTIONS

SECTION A
Finding Out About Forces

▲ St. Louis, Missouri, at night

The mighty Mississippi River flows past many cities and small towns. Along the river, you can see many bridges. They connect the banks and allow people to cross over the river. People planned the bridges carefully. The bridges had to hold up in heavy wind and in fast-moving waters. They had to carry many cars and trucks. To build a strong bridge, people needed to understand all the forces that could weaken it. What do you think some of these forces are? The investigations in this section can help you answer some of your questions about forces. You can keep notes in your Science Log.

▲ Swinging footbridge over a river in Zanskar, India

1 WHAT ARE FORCES?

You have heard the word *force* before. But what exactly is a force? Think about the many things you do. Do you ever use a force to help you do them? This lesson will give you a chance to explore forces. As you investigate, think about how you would define *force*. Later you can share your definition with your classmates.

Pushes and Pulls

You can move things by pushing them or pulling them. What do pushes and pulls have to do with force?

Jennifer is pulling her younger brother in a wagon. Would it be easier for her if she carried him? ▼

Mark is trying to score a goal. How did he get the ball rolling towards the net?

Chris is flying a kite. The wind pushes against the kite while Chris holds the string. If he doesn't keep pulling on the string, the kite will fly away. ▶

These students are having a tug-of-war contest. The team that pulls harder will win. ▼

How are all these situations alike? They all involve using a force to put an object in motion or to stop it from moving. A force can be used to get something going, as when you pull a wagon or kick a ball. It can also be used to keep something from moving, as when you hold onto a kite string.

Sometimes more than one force acts on the same object, as when two teams compete in a tug of war. The object may or may not move. It depends on how strong the forces are and whether they act in the same direction or in opposite directions.

Forces can be measured much as you measure length, width, and mass.

▲ Mass is measured in units of grams or kilograms, using a balance.

▲ Length and width are measured in units of centimeters or meters, using a ruler or a meter stick.

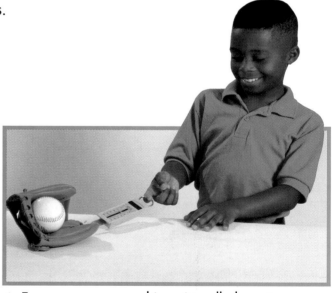

▲ Forces are measured in units called *newtons*. Spring scales are used to measure forces.

THINK ABOUT IT

How do forces cause things to move?

ACTIVITY

Measuring Forces

How can you measure the force it takes to move an eraser? Let's find out.

MATERIALS
- spring scale
- large plastic bag
- large eraser
- stapler
- Science Log data sheet

DO THIS

1. Work with a partner. Hook your finger on the hook of the spring scale. Have your partner hold the other end still. Look at the pointer on the scale. What happens when you pull on the scale?

2. Hold the hook still while your partner pulls the other end. What happens? If you want to change the reading on the scale, does it matter which person pulls?

3. Look at the numbers on the scale. Pull on the hook so that the scale reads 1 newton. Pull harder so that it reads 2 newtons. See how hard you have to pull to get the scale to read 6 newtons.

4 Make a chart like the one here.

5 Put the eraser in the plastic bag, and hook the bag on the scale. Use the scale to pull the bag across your desk. How many newtons does it take to pull it? Record your findings in the chart.

6 Repeat step 5. This time, put the stapler in the bag. Record the findings in your chart.

THINK AND WRITE

Suppose you used the spring scale to pull two boxes that are the same size across the floor. One of the boxes is empty, the other is filled with rocks. Which box would take more force to move? Why do you think so? What did you observe in this activity that supports your answer?

FORCE NEEDED TO MOVE ITEMS	
Item	Force
Eraser	
Stapler	

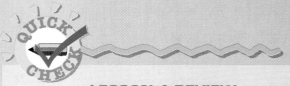

LESSON 1 REVIEW

Make a list of things you use every day that require a push or pull.

2 MAGNETS USE FORCE

Forces act to push and pull objects. When you push a box across the floor, you are touching the box. But some forces act between objects even when the objects aren't touching. Now you will investigate magnetism, one of these forces.

ACTIVITY

A Magnet and a Paper Clip

Magnets attract some types of metal. Will a magnet attract a paper clip if there is something between them?

MATERIALS
- 1-cm graph paper
- small paper clip
- bar magnet
- sheet of paper
- book
- Science Log data sheet

DO THIS

❶ Make a chart like the one below.

HOW FAR AWAY WAS THE MAGNET FROM THE PAPER CLIP?			
	Trial 1	Trial 2	Trial 3
Only Air Between Them			
Paper Between Them			
Book Between Them			

❷ Draw a line on one end of the graph paper.

3 Place the paper clip against the line. Place the bar magnet on the other end of the graph paper. Slowly slide the bar magnet toward the clip. Stop as soon as the clip moves. Count the number of squares between the magnet and the line you drew. Record your findings. Do the test two more times.

4 Repeat step 3. This time, hold a sheet of paper between the magnet and the paper clip. How far away is the magnet from the paper clip when the clip moves? Record your findings.

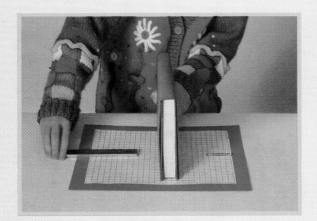

5 Repeat step 3 one more time. This time, hold a book between the magnet and the paper clip. Record your findings.

THINK AND WRITE

1. Does a magnet need to touch an object in order to move it? What observations did you make that support your answer?

2. **INFERRING** When you infer, you try to explain what you observed. In this activity, you observed the movement of a paper clip when you put a magnet near it. What can you infer about magnets, based on these observations?

C19

ACTIVITY

Two Magnets

Bar magnets have two ends. Usually the ends are marked in some way. Some magnets have a red end and a silver end. Other magnets have one end marked with an **N** and the other marked with an **S**. The **N** stands for *north,* and the **S** stands for *south.* Are there any differences between the two ends? In this activity, you will explore magnets and their ends.

MATERIALS

- 1-cm graph paper
- 2 bar magnets (with the ends marked)
- Science Log data sheet

DO THIS

1 Make a chart like the one below.

WHEN DID THE MAGNET MOVE?		
	Distance Apart	Direction It Moved
North to North		
South to North		
North to South		
South to South		

2 Place two bar magnets on the graph paper as shown. Draw a line on each end of the graph paper. Make sure one end of each magnet is against the line.

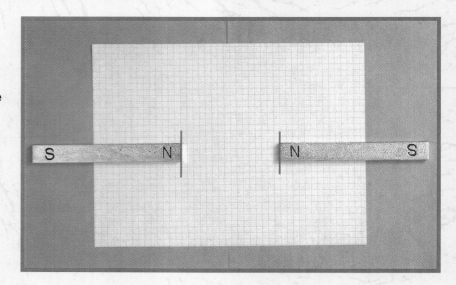

3 Slowly slide the magnet on the left toward the magnet on the right. Stop when the magnet on the right moves. Count the number of squares that were between the magnets when the magnet on the right started to move. Did it move toward the other magnet or away from it? Record your findings in the chart.

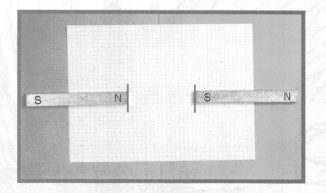

5 Place the magnets as shown above and repeat step 3.

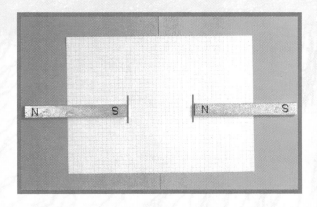

4 Set up the magnets again. This time, place them as shown above. Repeat step 3.

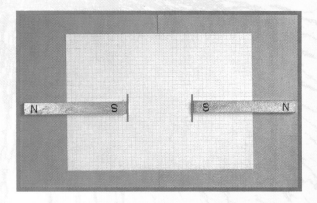

6 Now place the magnets as shown above and repeat step 3. Make sure you record your findings.

THINK AND WRITE

1. What happened when the similar ends of two magnets were near each other?

2. What happened when the different ends of two magnets were near each other?

Magnets in Our Lives

You know that magnets pull, or *attract*, certain metals. Because magnets do this, they can be very useful. Look at some ways people use magnets.

▲ Has anyone in your family attached one of your school papers to the refrigerator door? He or she may have used a magnet to hold the paper in place. In homes, small magnets are used for holding school papers and many other things in place.

▲ High-speed trains of the future, like this train in Japan, will use magnetism to zoom along tracks without touching them. Magnets underneath the train will push against, or *repel*, the magnets along the track. Because of this, the trains will ride about 10 centimeters (4 inches) above the track.

▲ Today, people don't have to worry about dropped screws. They can use a magnetic screwdriver to hold the screw in place.

A junkyard crane uses a powerful magnet to lift and move old cars and other large objects made of metal. ▼

Magnets are used in electric can openers to hold the lids once the cans are opened. What do you think would happen to the lids if there were no magnets to hold them? ▶

▲ Magnets are placed on some cabinet doors.

The doors close more easily and stay closed because of magnets. ▶

LESSON 2 REVIEW

1 Make a list of ways magnets are used in your home.

2 Think about the activity Two Magnets. The following sentences explain what happened. Rewrite these sentences in your own words, using the words *north* and *south*.

The like ends of two magnets push against, or repel, each other. The unlike ends of two magnets pull on, or attract, each other.

3 GRAVITY IS A FORCE

Magnets pull on only some things. On the following pages, you will investigate a force that acts between all objects—a force that bridge builders must always keep in mind.

ACTIVITY

Measuring Earth's Pull on Objects

Earth pulls on objects. You can measure that pull by using a spring scale.

DO THIS

❶ Make a chart like the one shown below.

FORCE NEEDED TO LIFT OBJECTS	
Object	Force

❷ Hold each object in your hand. Think about how much force it takes to lift each one. In the chart, list the objects in order. Start with the one that you think takes the most force to lift.

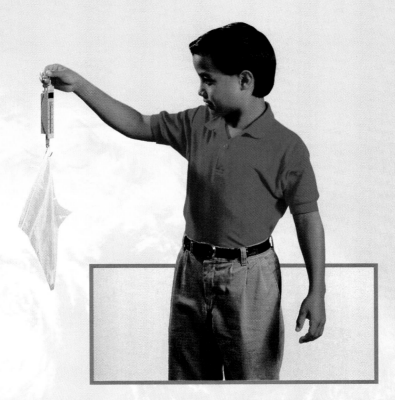

3 Put the stone into the plastic bag. Hook the bag onto the spring scale.

4 With the spring scale, lift the stone off the table. Record the number of newtons needed to lift the stone.

5 Repeat steps 3 and 4 with each of the other objects.

6 Choose other objects from around the classroom. Add them to your chart, and find out how much force it takes to lift them.

THINK AND WRITE

1. Look at your chart. Number the objects from the heaviest to the lightest. How accurate were your predictions? On what did you base your predictions? Why?

2. PREDICTING When you predict, you try to figure out what will happen in a certain situation. To predict, you use your observations and what you already know. What observations did you make at the beginning of this activity? How did these observations help you make your predictions?

You have measured Earth's pull on some objects. Read on to find out more about the force that causes Earth's pull.

In 1665, a young man left the city of London because of a sickness that was sweeping the city. He went to live in the country until the sickness was no longer a threat. This young man was a student of the sciences. He was still learning what scientists of his day knew about the natural world.

During his visit in the country, this young man made many observations about what he saw. He wrote down many questions about his observations. Actually, he did what scientists and students are still doing. He wondered.

One of the things this young man wondered about was why things fall. Why don't they float or go upward? This problem puzzled him greatly. He continued to work on a solution long after he returned to the city.

After considering this problem for some time, he came to the conclusion that Earth has a type of force that pulls objects toward it. The young man was Isaac Newton. He called this force *gravity*.

Every object on Earth, in our solar system, and in the universe has gravity. It holds us to the surface of Earth. Gravity even directs the movement of the stars and planets.

▲ **Isaac Newton**

In the activity you just did, you measured the force it took to lift an object. For example, to lift the book, you may have needed a force of 4 newtons. Earth's gravity was pulling on the book with a force of 4 newtons. This pull on the object is called its weight. **Weight** is the measure of the pull of gravity on an object. The book has weight because Earth's gravity is pulling on it. When you predicted which object would need the greatest force to be lifted, you probably based your prediction on which object was the heaviest.

▲ **Earth's gravity pulls a diver down to the pool.**

LESSON 3 REVIEW

How much would you weigh if there were no such force as gravity? Explain your answer.

C27

4 SHAPES AND THEIR STRENGTH

Gravity pulls on all things on Earth's surface. Therefore, bridges and other structures must be built so they will stand up to the pull of gravity. How do construction workers do this? Using strong materials like steel helps, but the real secret is in the design. Many shapes can be used in designs. Which ones are best?

ACTIVITY

Which Shape Is Strongest?

A well-designed structure can support heavy loads even if it's made out of something as flimsy as paper. Now you will have the chance to build your own paper structures and test their strength.

DO THIS

1 Fold one sheet of paper in half.

2 Fold another sheet of paper into thirds as shown. Tape the ends together.

3 Cut a third sheet of paper in half as shown. Fold each piece in half, and tape the pieces together as shown.

4 Roll another sheet around a metal can. Tape it so it will stay in the shape of a cylinder. Remove the container.

5 How should the paper structures be set on the desk so that they support the most books? Which shape do you think will support the most books? Study the shapes and record your predictions.

6 It's now time to test the shapes you have made. Set one of the shapes on your desk, and place a book on top of it. Does the shape support the book? Try setting the shape on the desk in several different ways. Which way works best? Record your observations. Then test the other shapes in the same way. Be sure to record your observations each time.

THINK AND WRITE

1. If you were building a bridge, which shapes might you use to support it? Tell why.

2. **EXPERIMENTING** One way to test, or check, an idea you have is to do an experiment. When you experiment, you make observations, ask a question, form a hypothesis, and design a test. Then you gather materials, do the test, and record the data. Finally, you look at the data and check to see if your hypothesis makes sense. In this activity, what were you trying to test?

7 Conduct a test to see which shape can hold the most books. Keep adding books to see how many each shape can hold. Record your observations.

Types of Bridges

A single sheet of paper can be folded in many ways to support a stack of books. Bridge builders have even more choices since there are many different materials they can use.

Long ago, bridges were built with whatever materials people could find—trees, vines, wood, and stone. These early bridges were simple structures, but they did the job. As time went by, the need for stronger bridges grew.

People found new and better ways of building bridges.

There is no "best" type of bridge. Different bridges are needed for different purposes. Some are built over large rivers, and others cross small streams. Some are built for trains to travel on, and others for people to walk across. Here are some examples of the many different types of bridges. How are they alike? How are they different?

▲ The Marco Polo Bridge in Beijing, China, is a *stone arch bridge*. It was built in 1192 and is over 235 meters (770 feet) long. Even though it is very old, it is still very sturdy. Buses, cars, trucks, and people still use this bridge today!

▲ The Golden Gate Bridge in San Francisco is one of the world's longest *suspension bridges*. In a suspension bridge, the road hangs from steel cables. The cables are supported by two high towers.

If you have ever driven on a highway, you have probably crossed over *girder bridges*. They are called that because they are made of steel beams called girders. ▶

The Warm Springs Bridge in Sonoma County, California, is a *truss bridge*. Small triangle-shaped sections help support the roadway. ▶

▲ This bridge in Porto, Portugal, is a *steel arch bridge*. The lower roadway hangs on girders under the arch. The upper roadway rests on girders on top of the arch.

▲ Look at this *cantilever bridge* in Canada. It goes across the St. Lawrence River in Quebec. It has two separate sections called cantilevers that extend from opposite banks of a river. The cantilevers are joined by a middle span. Most cantilever bridges are made of steel.

QUICK CHECK

LESSON 4 REVIEW

What types of bridges are there in your town or community? Make a sketch of a bridge near where you live, and add it to your Science Log. Identify the type of bridge.

DOUBLE CHECK

SECTION A REVIEW

1. Write the word *FORCE* inside a circle. Draw lines from the circle. Next to the lines, write words or sentences that tell what you have learned about forces in this section.

2. How are magnetism and gravity alike? How are they different? Write a paragraph comparing them.

What Causes Motion?

▲ **A freight train winds its way along the tracks in Squamish, British Columbia, in Canada.**

You slap a hockey puck with your stick, and the puck moves across the ice with amazing speed. A train slowly picks up speed as it pulls a long string of boxcars. Why is it sometimes easy to move an object and at other times much harder? What makes things move?

In this section, you'll investigate how some forces can make something move and how others can slow it down or stop it. Your investigations will help you understand why things move. Keep notes in your Science Log.

1 FORCES AND MOTION

Have you ever put down a pencil and found that it kept rolling away? Did you wonder why it moved? And why did it stay in one place when it finally stopped?

ACTIVITY

MATERIALS

- spiral notebook
- string (about 1 m)
- spring scale
- scissors
- Science Log data sheet

Balanced Forces

Now you have a chance to explore why objects move and why they stay still.

DO THIS

❶ Tie one end of the string to the spiral wire on the notebook.

❷ Tie the free end of the string to the spring scale. Let the notebook hang below the scale. Record the reading on the spring scale.

❸ Use the scissors to cut the string. What happens to the notebook? Record the reading on the spring scale again.

THINK AND WRITE

1. What forces kept the notebook hanging under the spring scale in step 2?

2. Why did the reading on the spring scale change in step 3?

3. Why did the notebook fall after you cut the string?

ACTIVITY

Forces Acting Together

You just saw what happens when forces act *against* each other. In this activity, you'll investigate what happens when forces act *together*.

DO THIS

1 Make a chart like this one.

SLIDING CUP	
Number of Strings	Time
1	
2	
3	

2 Bend the paper clip, and tape it to the cup as shown.

3 Tie one washer to the end of each string. Tie a loop at the other end of each string.

4 Place the cup on a table, 60 cm away from the edge. Mark the spot with a piece of tape. Put the remaining two washers in the cup. While your partner holds the cup, hook one of the strings onto the paper clip. The string should lie across the table, and the washer should hang over the edge.

C36

5 Now get the stopwatch ready. When your partner lets go of the cup, time how long it takes for the cup to slide to the edge of the table. Record the time in the chart.

6 Put the cup back where it started on the table. Add a second string and washer to the paper clip and repeat step 5. Then do this again with all three strings and washers.

THINK AND WRITE

1. Study the information you recorded in your chart. What can you conclude about several forces acting together on an object?

2. **INFERRING** When you infer, you use what you have observed to explain what has happened. In this activity, you observed what happened to a cup when extra mass was attached to the cup. Based on your observations, what can you infer about why the cup moved?

LESSON 1 REVIEW

Suppose you had a string with a washer tied to each end. What would happen if you hung the washers off opposite ends of a table? Explain your answer.

2 FRICTION

Most forces can speed things up or slow them down. Earth's gravity, for instance, can make an apple fall to the ground. It can also slow down a ball thrown upward into the air. But there are other forces that affect motion, too.

ACTIVITY

Make It Stop

There is a force that can make things slow down or stop. It can't make them move faster. In this activity, you'll investigate this force.

DO THIS

1 Make a chart like this one.

DISTANCE THE MARBLE TRAVELED			
Material	Trial 1	Trial 2	Trial 3
Wax Paper			
Sandpaper			
Bath Towel			

MATERIALS
- book
- wooden board (about 1 m long)
- wax paper (60 cm long)
- masking tape
- marble
- measuring tape
- several sheets of sandpaper taped together (60 cm long)
- bath towel
- Science Log data sheet

2 Place the book on the floor. Put one end of the board on the book to make a ramp. Lay the wax paper on the floor, at the bottom of the ramp. Tape it in place.

3 Place the marble at the top of the ramp, and let it go. Do not push it. Let it roll down the ramp and onto the wax paper.

4 Measure the distance from the bottom of the ramp to where the marble stops. Record the distance.

5 Do steps 3 and 4 two more times. Record your results each time.

6 Replace the wax paper with the sandpaper. Repeat steps 3–5, and record your results. Then replace the sandpaper with the towel, and repeat steps 3–5 once more. Record your results.

THINK AND WRITE

1. Look at your data. Over which surface did the marble travel the greatest distance? Over which surface did it travel the least distance?

2. Which material has the smoothest surface? Which has the roughest surface? How did the surfaces affect how far the marble rolled?

Looking Back   The marble rubs against anything it rolls on. It rubs very lightly against some surfaces and harder against others. In the activity, the marble rubbed against the wax paper the least and against the towel the most. Rubbing against the surface slowed the marble down. Some surfaces slow down an object more than others.

ACTIVITY

Make It Go

Smooth and rough surfaces can slow down a marble that is rolling across them. The marble you used was very smooth. Would the marble have gone as far if it had a rougher surface? Does the surface of an object affect how well it slides? Do the following investigation to find out.

MATERIALS
- rubber eraser
- small cardboard box
- coin
- cookie sheet
- Science Log data sheet

DO THIS

1 Examine the surfaces of the eraser, the box, and the coin. On your data sheet, describe the surface of each object. Predict which of the objects will slide the fastest on the cookie sheet and which will slide the slowest. Record your predictions.

2 Place the eraser, the box, and the coin along one edge of the cookie sheet. Raise this edge slowly until the objects begin to move. Which object moves first? Which moves last?

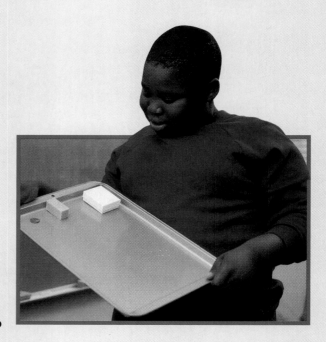

THINK AND WRITE

1. Tell how the surface of an object affects the way it moves.

2. **PREDICTING** When you predict, you try to figure out what will happen in a certain situation. What observations and experiences did you use to predict which object would slide first and which would slide last?

C40

What Is Friction?

In the activities, you explored how objects moved on different surfaces. Why do objects sometimes slow down as they move?

When one object moves over the surface of another, the two surfaces rub against each other and a force is produced. **Friction** is the force that causes objects to slow down or stop. Different surfaces produce different amounts of friction. The following photos show friction at work. They also show ways to reduce friction.

▲ These children are sledding. They can zoom down the snowy hill because there is very little friction between the sled and the snow.

Many of the parts in a car's engine rub against each other. If there is too much friction, the parts wear out faster. People add oil to their cars to reduce the friction between the parts. Since oil is very slippery, the parts slide smoothly against each other. ▶

In the winter, cars can skid on icy roads. Sand is sometimes put on the roads to increase the friction. In some places, people put chains on their tires to increase friction. ▼

◀ These tire chains increase friction, so the tires grip the road and the car doesn't slide on the ice.

This cardboard box is difficult to move because of the friction between the box and the sidewalk. How could you reduce the friction? ▶

Many bicycles have brake pads that rub against the wheel. Usually the pads are made of rubber. ▼

◀ The greater the friction between the pad and the wheel, the easier it is to stop the bike. What do you think would happen if the wheels or the brake pads got wet?

QUICK CHECK

LESSON 2 REVIEW

Explain how friction can be a very useful force. How can friction be a problem?

3 INVESTIGATING INERTIA

Suppose you're trying to push a car down the street by yourself. You push with all your might, but the car doesn't move. You're not strong enough to overcome the force of friction between the car and the road. If there were no friction between the car and the road, you could push the car, but it still wouldn't be easy. To find out why, read the text, do the activities, and look at the photos on the following pages.

What Is Inertia?

To answer this question, read on.

One of the astronauts who went to the moon took along a golf ball. He placed the ball on the surface of the moon. It would have remained there for a very long time if it hadn't been disturbed. But the astronaut had also taken a golf club. He hit the ball with a good, hard swing. The ball flew up and kept going and going—much farther than it would have on Earth. The pull of gravity is much less on the moon than it is on Earth. But the moon's gravity was strong enough to make the ball finally come back down. What if there had been no gravity to pull it down? The ball would have flown through space forever unless it hit something.

▲ Astronaut Alan B. Shepard on the moon

An object doesn't move unless a force moves it. If it is moving, it keeps moving until another force stops it. This is a property that all objects have. It is called *inertia* (in UR shuh).

▲ The things in a room don't move unless someone or something moves them.

After you leave for school in the morning, your bed, dresser, desk, and chair stay in place. When you come home, they're all still in place unless someone has moved them. What would life be like if your bedroom furniture could move around on its own?

Suppose you're riding your bicycle. You've pedaled hard and are going at a fairly good speed. Suddenly you stop pedaling. What happens? The bicycle keeps going because objects that are moving tend to keep moving. Why doesn't it keep going forever? Friction slows down the bicycle. Unless you start pedaling again, friction will stop the bicycle.

▲ Bikes keep moving even after you stop pedaling because of inertia.

THINK ABOUT IT

Write a paragraph that describes what a trip from home to school would be like if the force of friction were very small. Then write another paragraph that describes what the trip would be like if the force of friction were very large.

C45

ACTIVITY

It's Hard to Stop

When you ride in a car, your body moves just as fast as the car. If the car stops very suddenly, what happens? You can make a model to find out.

MATERIALS

- wooden board (about 1 m long)
- 5–7 books
- masking tape
- toy car
- 6 large washers
- safety goggles
- measuring tape
- Science Log data sheet

DO THIS

❶ Make a chart like the one below.

HOW FAR THE WASHERS WENT	
Number of Washers	Distance
2	
3	
4	

❷ Make a ramp about 8 cm to 10 cm high on the floor. Do this by placing one end of the board on two or three of the books. Use two books to form a wall at the bottom of the ramp.

❸ Tape two washers together. Place them on top of the car.

4 **CAUTION: Anyone near the car must wear safety goggles.** Put on the safety goggles. Release the car from the top of the ramp. Do not push the car.

5 When the washers land, measure how far they are from the car. Record your observations.

6 Use the tape to fasten another washer to the ones you used.

7 Repeat steps 4–6 until all six washers have been used.

THINK AND WRITE

1. What happened to the washers? Why do you think this happened?

2. Use your observations to explain why people use seat belts in cars.

3. **FORMULATING AND USING MODELS** Models are used to learn about objects or events that are difficult to study in real life. How could you use this model to study car crashes and ways to make cars safer? Why would you want to use this model rather than real cars?

ACTIVITY

Which Way Does It Go?

You can't see forces. You can only see what they do. In this activity, you'll make observations to figure out when forces are at work and when they aren't.

DO THIS

1 Put the marble inside the box. Have it touch the right side of the box.

2 Predict how the marble will move if you slide the box to the right. Try it. What happens?

3 Now predict how the marble will move if you slide the box to the left. Try it. What happens?

4 Put the marble in the middle of the box. How will the marble move if you move the box away from you? Try it. What happens?

5 Try other positions in the box. Before you move the box each time, predict how the marble will move.

6 Record your observations.

THINK AND WRITE

Describe how the marble moved. Explain why it moved that way. When were forces acting on it, and when were they not?

Inertia and You

Inertia affects everything. Sometimes we even need protection from inertia. Some of the common things around us were invented to protect us from the effects of inertia.

▲ When a loaded fruit cart stops suddenly, the fruit keeps moving because of inertia. When an object stops suddenly, any unattached item in or on the object will keep moving.

◄ Handrails in a subway train help people balance themselves when the train moves or stops suddenly. When the train starts, the passengers move backward. When the train stops, they continue moving forward in the train.

Without a Seat Belt or an Air Bag

1. What happens when a person is in a stopped car and the driver presses down on the gas pedal? The seat pushes her forward.

2. If the car stops suddenly in a crash, she keeps moving forward.

3. She flies into the steering wheel and the windshield.

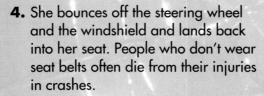

4. She bounces off the steering wheel and the windshield and lands back into her seat. People who don't wear seat belts often die from their injuries in crashes.

With a Seat Belt

1.

2.

3.

4.

Seat belts and air bags are designed to prevent you from hitting the dashboard or the windshield if the car stops suddenly in an accident.

With a Seat Belt and an Air Bag

1.

2.

3.

4.

QUICK CHECK

LESSON 3 REVIEW

Define *inertia* in your own words.

✓ DOUBLE CHECK

SECTION B REVIEW

1. You hit a ball into the air. There is a strong wind blowing toward you. Will the ball travel as far as it would on a calm day? What forces act on a ball that's hit on a windy day?

2. Large trucks often take longer to speed up or slow down than small cars do. Use what you have learned about inertia to explain why this is so.

SECTION C
Machines

The construction site is filled with activity. In one area, a crane gracefully lifts a steel beam to workers on a platform high above. The workers will carefully fit the beam into place. In another area, a truck is unloading cement. Workers push stacks of bricks up a ramp. Ropes and pulleys are used to carry materials to workers several stories up. "Look at all those machines!" says a man watching from the sidewalk.

Why do people use machines, and how do machines help us build things? How do machines push, pull, lift, and carry things? In this section, you will discover answers to these and other questions as you explore machines. Keep notes in your Science Log.

1 LEVERS

Many machines that are used in construction are complex and very new. But there are other machines that are much simpler and have been used for thousands of years. In this lesson, you will investigate one of these machines.

What Is a Lever?

A man is trying to get a large rock out of the ground. He tries to push it and to pull it, but it is too heavy. What can he do?

He could get help from other people, or he could use a machine. He decides to use a machine called a *lever.*

People have invented a number of machines to help them do things. A **machine** is a tool that changes either the amount of force acting on an object or the direction of the force. Some machines have many moving parts. Others have no moving parts or only a few and are called *simple machines.*

Using a lever is a simple way of lifting heavy things more easily. A **lever** is just a bar that rests on a point. The point the bar rests on is called a *fulcrum* (FUL kruhm). By placing the object to be moved at one end of the bar and pushing down on the other end, you can raise the object.

◄ Levers make it seem easier to do some things.

▲ **A seesaw is a lever.**

▲ **Crowbar**

Bottle opener ▶

You probably use levers every day without even knowing it. If you have ever used a stick to pry a rock out of the ground, then you have used a lever.

Have you ever played on a seesaw? One person goes up, while the other goes down. When you ride a seesaw, you are using a simple machine. The machine is a lever. Think about it. On a seesaw, your weight is lifting the other person up.

A bottle opener is a lever. It may not seem like much of a machine, but it would be very hard to open some bottles without it. Crowbars and nutcrackers are also levers.

THINK ABOUT IT

What are some examples of levers that you have used?

▲ **Nutcracker**

ACTIVITY

Using Levers

Now that you know what a lever is, you may be wondering how it works. To find out, do this activity.

DO THIS

1 Place one eraser on top of the other eraser. Make a lever by placing the meter stick on the erasers. The erasers will be the fulcrum. Place the erasers 20 cm from one end of the meter stick. Place the book on the opposite end.

2 Push down on the end of the meter stick opposite the book. Notice how hard you have to push to lift the book.

3 Move the fulcrum 10 cm closer to the book. Repeat step 2.

4 Move the fulcrum another 10 cm closer to the book, and repeat step 2. Keep moving the fulcrum closer to the book and repeating step 2.

MATERIALS
- 2 chalkboard erasers
- meter stick
- thin book
- Science Log data sheet

THINK AND WRITE

What conclusion can you make about the effect moving the fulcrum has on how the lever works?

Other Types of Levers

The lever you made is just one type of lever. Read about two other types of levers on these two pages.

Picture yourself fishing in a lake. Suddenly your rod dips. You have a bite! Quickly you begin to turn the handle on your reel. You are thinking about how big the fish is. It is giving you a good fight. Finally you reel the fish in. You probably never give much thought to the machine that helps you do this.

A fishing rod has a wheel and axle. The wheel and axle on your rod makes it easier for you to bring in the fish. You use less force than you would if you tried to pull the fish from the bottom of the lake without the wheel and axle.▶

The axle is the part of the rod that the fishing line is wound around. The wheel is the handle you turn. The longer the handle, the less force you need. But with the longer handle, you have to turn the wheel through a bigger circle. ▶

The wheel and axle is a type of lever. When you turn the handle one way, the bucket gets pulled up. This is similar to what happens with a lever that is like a seesaw. A wheel and axle can change the strength of a turning force. ▶

Another kind of lever is the pulley. You may have seen workers at a construction site using pulleys to raise things like buckets. A *pulley* is made of rope, string, or wire wound around a reel. ▶

The pulley is a type of lever. When you pull down on one end of the rope, the other end moves upward. This is similar to what happens with a lever that is like a seesaw. A single pulley can change the direction of a force. ▼

◀ Cranes have a heavy wire rope, called a *cable,* that passes through a group of pulleys.

THINK ABOUT IT

Write a paragraph explaining how the wheel and axle or the pulley is a lever.

Pulling with a Pulley

Pulleys make it seem easier to move heavy loads. See how easy it is by doing this activity.

- 2 broom handles
- rope (about 6 m long)
- Science Log data sheet

DO THIS

1 Tie one end of the rope to one of the broom handles. Make sure the knot is near one end of the broom handle.

2 Give the broom handle with the rope tied to it to one of your partners. Give the other broom handle to your other partner.

3 Have your two partners face each other and loop the rope around the broom handles several times as shown.

4 Have your partners try to hold the broom handles apart while you slowly pull on the free end of the rope. What happens?

THINK AND WRITE

Write a paragraph or draw a diagram explaining how you could use several pulleys to lift a heavy box off the ground.

QUICK CHECK

LESSON 1 REVIEW

Some workers are using a lever to lift heavy rocks. After lifting several, they try to lift one rock that is heavier, but they cannot lift it. What would you suggest they do to the lever so that they could lift the rock?

2 INCLINED PLANES

A woman is struggling to pull a baby carriage up the front steps to her apartment. She is having a difficult time getting it up the stairs. "I wish we had a ramp here!" she cries out in frustration.

What Is an Inclined Plane?

What is a ramp? Why would a ramp make it easier to move the carriage up to the front door?

An **inclined plane** is a flat surface that is raised at one end. Like the lever, it is a simple machine. The most common type of inclined plane is a ramp. Where have you seen ramps being used?

At construction sites, materials are often moved to higher levels by loading them onto a cart or a wheelbarrow and pushing them up a ramp. You may even prefer to walk up a ramp rather than take the stairs.

▲ Ramps are often used at construction sites.

Some things would be very difficult to do without using an inclined plane. ▼

THINK ABOUT IT

Why do you think there are laws that require buildings to have ramps or elevators for people who use wheelchairs?

ACTIVITY

Moving Up

Now let's use what you know about inclined planes.

DO THIS

❶ Make a chart like this.

FORCE NEEDED TO MOVE OBJECT		
	Without Ramp	With Ramp
Force		
Distance		

MATERIALS
- wooden board (about 1 m long)
- chair
- masking tape
- thin spiral notebook
- spring scale
- piece of string (30 cm long)
- meter stick
- Science Log data sheet

❷ Place one end of the board on the edge of the chair. Let the other end rest on the floor. Tape the board to the floor to hold it in place.

❸ Tie one end of the string to the spiral wire on the notebook. Tie the other end of the string to the hook on the spring scale.

❹ Do not use the ramp for this step. Place the notebook on the floor. Slowly and steadily begin lifting the notebook straight up off the floor while watching the spring scale. When the notebook is no longer touching the floor, read the setting on the spring scale. Continue raising the notebook until it is as high as the seat of the chair. Record the number of newtons needed to raise it.

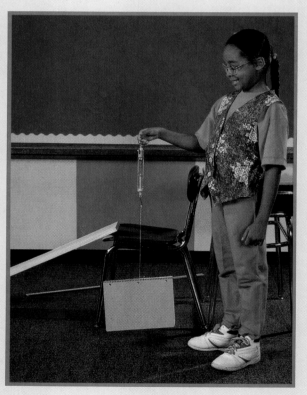

5 Measure the height you raised the notebook. Record this distance.

6 Now place the notebook on the floor near the bottom end of the ramp. Slowly and steadily begin pulling the spring scale up the ramp. When the notebook begins moving, read the setting on the spring scale. Continue to pull the notebook until it reaches the top of the ramp. Record the number of newtons needed to pull it up the ramp.

7 Measure the length of the ramp, and record this distance.

THINK AND WRITE

1. Which method of moving the book required more force?

2. Which method of moving the book required moving it a greater distance?

3. In what ways did the ramp help you lift the book? What did you have to give up in order to get that help?

4. **EXPERIMENTING** You often make observations about things that happen around you. Sometimes you have a question about something you have observed. To answer your question, you may design a test. Now that you have studied some simple machines, design a test to find the easiest way to move three boxes of books from the second floor to the first floor.

Wedges and Screws

A ramp is one kind of inclined plane, but it isn't the only kind. Inclined planes can also be used to cut objects and to hold objects together.

An ax, with an inclined plane on both sides, is used for splitting wood. This type of inclined plane is called a *wedge*. The shape of an ax makes it easier to push apart the log into two pieces. ▶

◀ A plow is another example of a wedge that farmers have used for hundreds of years. As it is dragged through a field, the plow cuts through the soil and moves it aside.

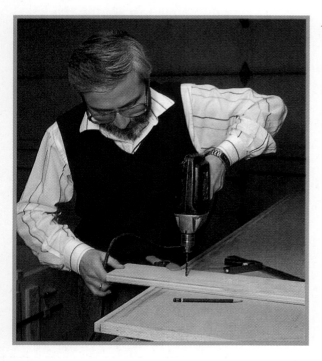

◀ The screw is another kind of inclined plane. Usually, you think of using screws to fasten things together, but there are other uses for a screw. Drills use a kind of screw called a *bit* to make holes in objects. Some screws can be used to lift things.

THINK ABOUT IT

Draw a diagram to show how an ax is an inclined plane.

Making a Model of a Screw

Where is the inclined plane on a screw? This activity should help you answer that question.

DO THIS

1. Cut the sheet of paper in half.

2. Use the ruler to draw a thick, straight line across one of the halves from one corner to the opposite corner.

3. Cut along the line. You now have two inclined planes.

4. Wrap one inclined plane around the pencil. Start with the shortest side of the triangle. What does your pencil look like?

MATERIALS

- sheet of construction paper
- scissors
- ruler
- pencil
- Science Log data Sheet

THINK AND WRITE

Where can you find an inclined plane on a screw?

QUICK CHECK

LESSON 2 REVIEW

How are the ramp and the screw alike? How are they different?

3 COMPOUND MACHINES

You've had a chance to investigate and even construct some simple machines. But wait, there's more! Now you'll have a chance to see how they can be combined.

What Is a Compound Machine?

Just as you might have thought, it is possible to put two or more simple machines together. By doing this, you make a compound machine.

Compound machines allow us to do difficult and complex jobs more easily. But sometimes compound machines are used for what seem like simple jobs, such as opening a can. You can get a good idea about what compound machines are like from the pictures you see here.

▲ This can opener is a compound machine made up of a lever, a wedge, and a wheel and axle.

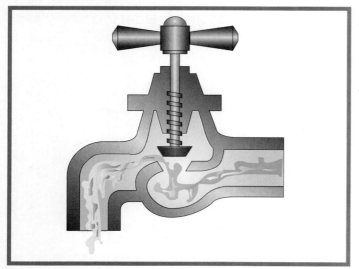

◄ A faucet uses the combination of a screw and a wheel and axle to control the flow of water.

A farm combine is used to harvest crops such as wheat and oats. It is made up of many simple machines. ▼

Screws called *augers* pull wheat kernels up and into a storage bin.

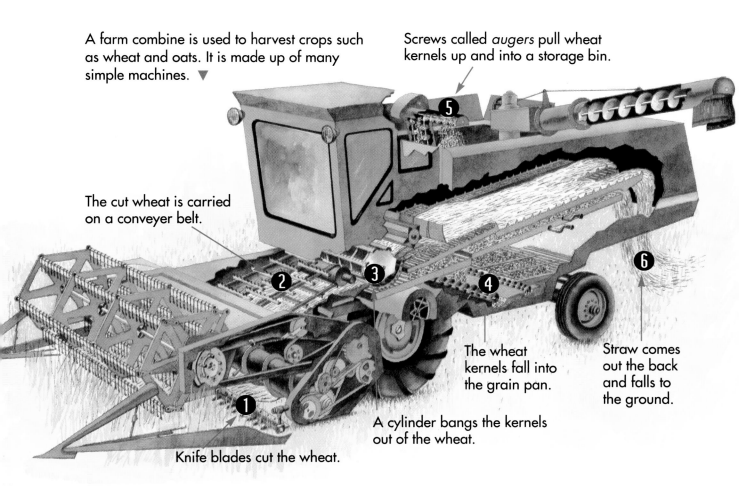

The cut wheat is carried on a conveyer belt.

⑤

②

③

④

⑥

The wheat kernels fall into the grain pan.

Straw comes out the back and falls to the ground.

①

A cylinder bangs the kernels out of the wheat.

Knife blades cut the wheat.

This machine is called a bucket wheel excavator (EHK skuh vayt uhr). It is used in construction for digging on the surface. It is so complex that more than ten people are needed to operate it. ▼

THINK ABOUT IT

Look at the combine and the bucket wheel excavator. How many simple machines can you identify?

Cindy Del Arroyo
Heavy-Equipment Operator

As you might think, it requires a great deal of skill to operate some types of construction equipment. Now you can read about a woman who has and uses this skill.

▲ **Cindy Del Arroyo**

Cindy Del Arroyo operates heavy equipment. Before beginning this career, she served in the United States Marine Corps and then spent several years on the security force at a power plant. Later, Del Arroyo was a postal carrier.

Finally, she decided that she really wanted to become a construction worker. She took the test to work for CALTRANS, the California Department of Transportation, which builds, repairs, and maintains the roads in California.

Ms. Del Arroyo passed the test, and the people at CALTRANS were impressed by her previous experience because it showed that she was a responsible person. They asked her to take a course on driving heavy equipment. After two weeks of intensive training, Del Arroyo was ready to start her job as a heavy-equipment operator. The rest of her training has been on the job. Today she is perfectly at ease driving a loader or a truck.

Del Arroyo operating a loader ▶

In California, there are lots of mountains near the highways. Sometimes a mudslide blocks a road completely. Then Ms. Del Arroyo has to use her loader to clear a path.

A heavy-equipment operator has to have steady nerves. Working on a highway can be dangerous, but Del Arroyo is not bothered by this. She likes the challenge her job presents and the variety of tasks she has to do. There's never a dull moment!

Del Arroyo and her family ▼

The skills Del Arroyo has learned are shared with her family. Her four-year-old son has his own little toy loader in the back yard, and her husband uses heavy equipment in his landscaping business.

Ms. Del Arroyo hopes more women will consider construction jobs in the future. She says that common sense and a desire to do a job well are needed for this career. When she is asked what her experience has taught her, her face lights up and she replies, "I always say you can do whatever you want to. You just have to stick with it!" Cindy Del Arroyo is living proof of that.

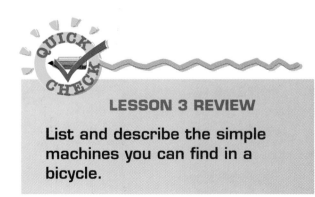

LESSON 3 REVIEW

List and describe the simple machines you can find in a bicycle.

4 BUILDING BRIDGES

Machines allow people to build things that would be impossible to build without them. Still, there are limits to what machines can do. The people who design bridges, buildings, and other structures have to work within these limits. However, with a great deal of planning, they can accomplish things that seem impossible.

The BRIDGE That Couldn't be BUILT

by **Mel Boring**
from *Cricket*

Born on New York's Lower East Side, David B. Steinman grew up in the shadow of the famous Brooklyn Bridge. When he was ten and selling newspapers, he'd often point to the structure and tell the other newsboys that he was going to build bridges like it someday. They just laughed.

But David did go on to fulfill his dream. Over the next fifty years, he worked on the designs of 400 bridges all over the world. And one of his greatest challenges was the Mackinac Bridge that spans the four-mile-wide straits between Upper and Lower Michigan.

▲ **David B. Steinman**

In 1950, when the state of Michigan decided to build the bridge, the committee in charge considered three famous construction engineers for the job. They ended up choosing David B. Steinman.

Steinman was an experienced engineer, yet most people thought that even he would be unable to bridge the Straits of Mackinac. Why did they think the job was impossible? For one reason, the weather in the straits is some of the worst in the world. There Lake Michigan flows into Lake Huron through a narrow neck of water—one Great Lake emptying into another the size of a small ocean. In the winter the weather in the straits gets downright nasty. Winds have been known to blow 78 miles per hour. That much wind can whip up 50-foot waves. The seesaw winds, plus the swift flow of water between the two Great Lakes, pile the ice high in the straits until the water becomes a mass of jumbled, jagged ice. The ice, three and four feet thick, bumps and grinds against everything in its path—including bridges.

But David Steinman was determined to go ahead, and in February 1954 he began building his suspension bridge. A suspension bridge is one whose roadway hangs from huge cables. The cables are supported by high towers sunk deep into the bedrock beneath the water.

Steinman used many of the usual bridge-building techniques of the day,

▼ This view of the Great Lakes shows how the Mackinac Bridge connects the two parts of Michigan.

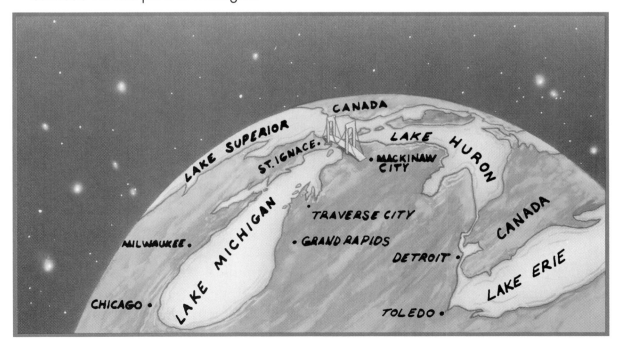

▲ **The Mackinac Bridge**

but then he added new ideas of his own. Those high winds in the straits could blow with a force of up to 20 pounds on every square foot of the bridge. Steinman multiplied that number by two and a half so that the bridge would withstand forces of 50 pounds per square foot. He also designed part of the roadway with grates—steel sheets with holes in them—so that the wind would blow through the bridge, rather than just against it.

As many as 1,000 people worked on the bridge at one time, building a structure able to withstand more ice pressure than the Mackinac Straits would ever push upon it. In his laboratory testing, David Steinman found that his bridge model would withstand 23,000 pounds of ice pressure on each linear foot of steel. David multiplied that by five so that each foot of steel in the finished bridge could withstand 115,000 pounds of ice.

David Steinman grew worried when the Mackinac Bridge faced its first real-life test. The final winter of its construction was called "the champion of bad winters." Winds above 70 miles per hour flung icebergs through the Mackinac channels, smashing against the nearly finished

bridge. Temperatures plunged to 40° below zero, and geysers of spray froze four stories high on the towers. But the Mackinac Bridge withstood the test, convincing many of the skeptics that Steinman's suspension bridge, the longest ever built, would stay put. Even engineers who said it would be impossible to build now believe that the bridge will last at least 1,000 years.

The "Big Mac" opened to cars right on schedule on November 1, 1957, and for the first time ever, travelers could drive between Michigan's upper and lower peninsulas. Over 2.5 million cars cross the bridge every year.

If you ever travel from Lower Michigan to Upper Michigan, from Mackinaw City on the south side of the straits to St. Ignace on the north, you can ride over the Big Mac. And when you do, you'll probably understand why people said the bridge could never be built. By the time David Steinman died in August 1960, however, Michiganites were calling the Big Mac "the bridge that couldn't be built but was"!

THINK ABOUT IT

What forces did David Steinman have to consider when he designed and built the "Big Mac" bridge?

Building Your Own Bridge

David Steinman designed and built many bridges. Now it's your turn.

DO THIS

1 With your partner, design and draw a diagram of a bridge. As you plan your design, keep in mind the following rules.

MATERIALS

- 25 craft sticks
- 100 toothpicks
- white glue
- brick
- stopwatch
- 6–8 books
- Science Log data sheet

RULES

- You must use only the materials you are given.
- The bridge you build must be able to span a gap of 25 cm.
- The bridge must touch only the top surfaces of the supports.
- The bridge must be able to support the weight of a brick for at least 5 seconds.
- The bridge must be able to support the brick at all points along the span.

2 Once you have designed your bridge, begin building it using the craft sticks, toothpicks, and glue. Make sure you wait overnight for the glue to dry.

3 To test your bridge, set it on two stacks of books that are 25 cm apart. Then gently place a brick on the span of the bridge, and let it rest there for 5 seconds. Good luck!

THINK AND WRITE

1. Write a paragraph explaining how you designed and built your bridge. What worked in your design and what did not? How could you improve your design?

2. **FORMULATING AND USING MODELS** When building a model, you need to think about many of the same things you would have to consider if you were building a real structure. But there are also some things that are different. Suppose you were building a real bridge. What things would you have to consider that you did not have to consider in this activity?

LESSON 4 REVIEW

When David Steinman was working on the "Big Mac" bridge, he designed it to withstand forces much greater than he thought it would have to face. Why do you think he made it stronger than seemed necessary?

 DOUBLE CHECK

SECTION C REVIEW

1. Suppose you were trying to load a heavy box into the back of a car. Describe two different ways you could use simple machines.

2. Suppose you were building a bridge. Write a paragraph explaining how you would use simple machines to help you build the bridge.

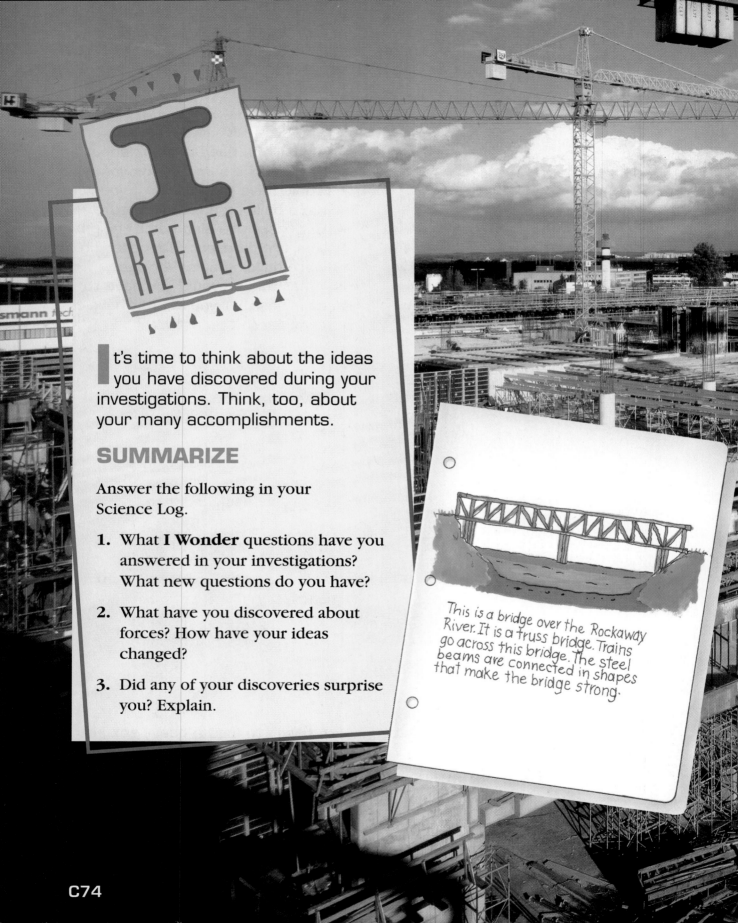

I REFLECT

It's time to think about the ideas you have discovered during your investigations. Think, too, about your many accomplishments.

SUMMARIZE

Answer the following in your Science Log.

1. What **I Wonder** questions have you answered in your investigations? What new questions do you have?

2. What have you discovered about forces? How have your ideas changed?

3. Did any of your discoveries surprise you? Explain.

This is a bridge over the Rockaway River. It is a truss bridge. Trains go across this bridge. The steel beams are connected in shapes that make the bridge strong.

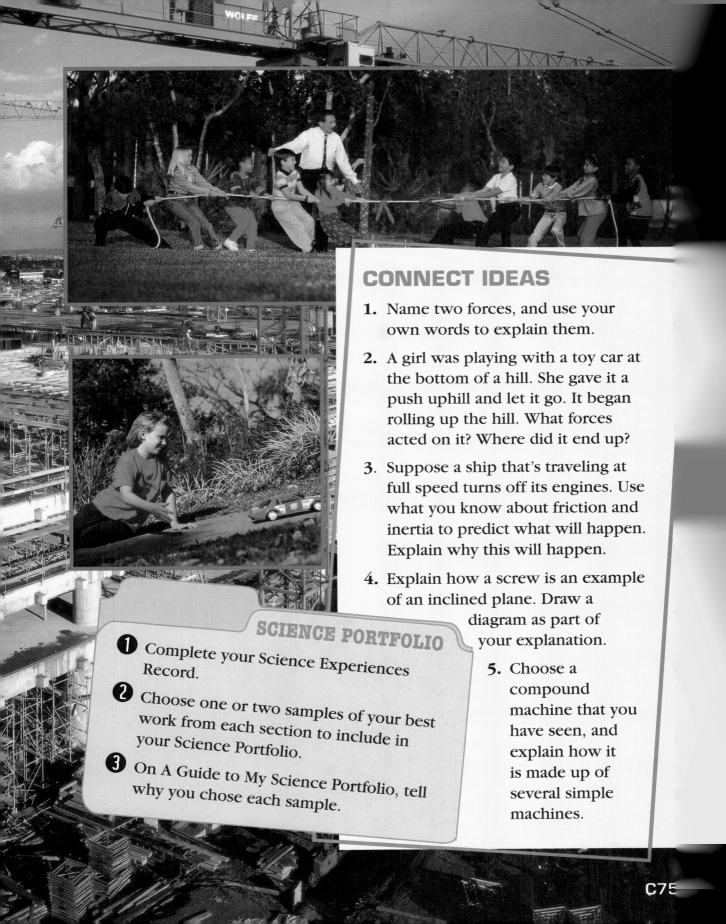

CONNECT IDEAS

1. Name two forces, and use your own words to explain them.

2. A girl was playing with a toy car at the bottom of a hill. She gave it a push uphill and let it go. It began rolling up the hill. What forces acted on it? Where did it end up?

3. Suppose a ship that's traveling at full speed turns off its engines. Use what you know about friction and inertia to predict what will happen. Explain why this will happen.

4. Explain how a screw is an example of an inclined plane. Draw a diagram as part of your explanation.

5. Choose a compound machine that you have seen, and explain how it is made up of several simple machines.

SCIENCE PORTFOLIO

❶ Complete your Science Experiences Record.

❷ Choose one or two samples of your best work from each section to include in your Science Portfolio.

❸ On A Guide to My Science Portfolio, tell why you chose each sample.

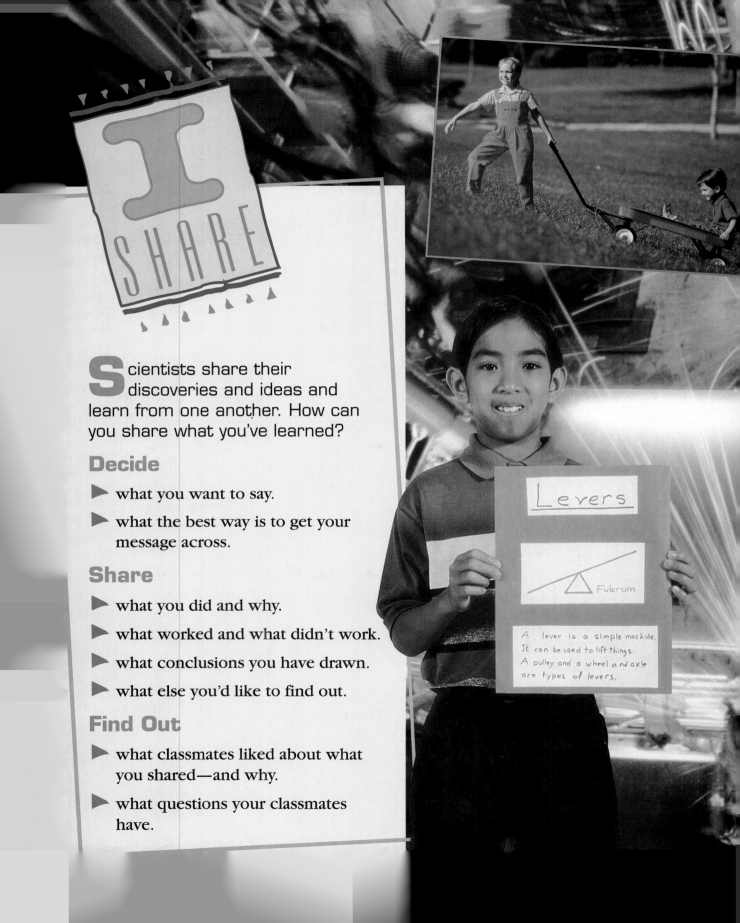

I SHARE

Scientists share their discoveries and ideas and learn from one another. How can you share what you've learned?

Decide

▶ what you want to say.

▶ what the best way is to get your message across.

Share

▶ what you did and why.

▶ what worked and what didn't work.

▶ what conclusions you have drawn.

▶ what else you'd like to find out.

Find Out

▶ what classmates liked about what you shared—and why.

▶ what questions your classmates have.

Levers

Fulcrum

A lever is a simple machine.
It can be used to lift things.
A pulley and a wheel and axle
are types of levers.

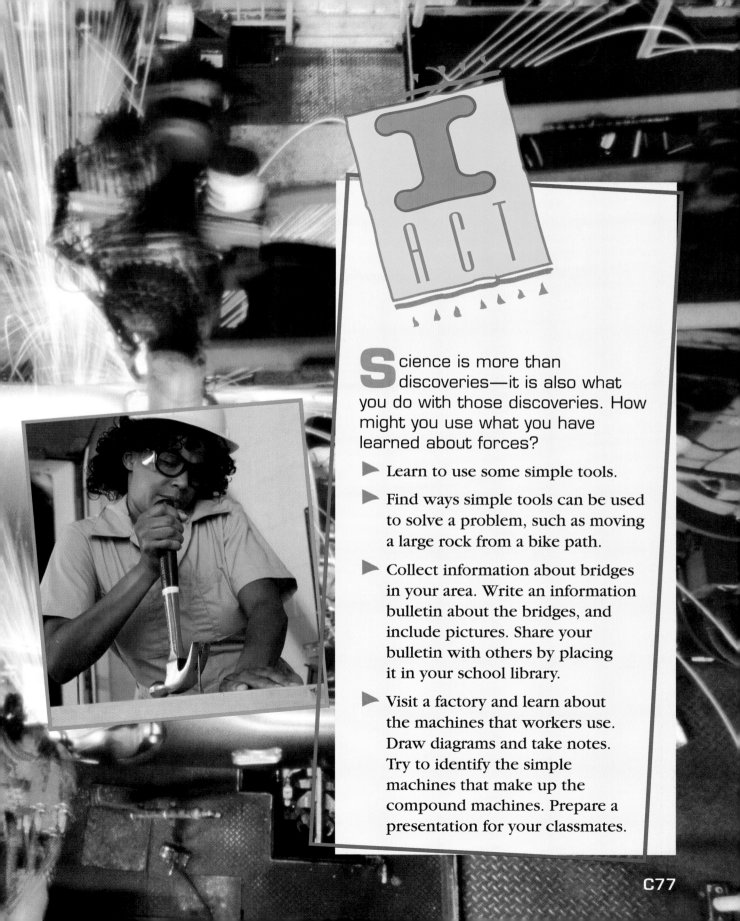

I ACT

Science is more than discoveries—it is also what you do with those discoveries. How might you use what you have learned about forces?

▶ Learn to use some simple tools.

▶ Find ways simple tools can be used to solve a problem, such as moving a large rock from a bike path.

▶ Collect information about bridges in your area. Write an information bulletin about the bridges, and include pictures. Share your bulletin with others by placing it in your school library.

▶ Visit a factory and learn about the machines that workers use. Draw diagrams and take notes. Try to identify the simple machines that make up the compound machines. Prepare a presentation for your classmates.

THE LANGUAGE OF SCIENCE

The language of science helps people communicate clearly when they talk about forces, motion, and machines. Here are some vocabulary words you can use when you talk about forces, motion, and machines with friends, family, and others.

compound machine—a combination of two or more simple machines. For instance, a can opener is a compound machine made up of a lever, a wheel and axle, and a wedge. **(C64)**

▲ Can Opener

force—a push or a pull. **(C15)**

friction—a force that acts between any two objects that are touching or rubbing against each other. Friction slows or stops movement. **(C41)**

gravity—the force that pulls all objects toward each other. A very massive object, such as Earth, pulls on another object, such as a rock, with a greater force than less massive objects, such as a baseball, pulls on the rock. **(C26)**

▲ Gravity pulls this diver into the pool.

inclined plane—a simple machine that has a surface set at an angle. An inclined plane connects a lower place to a higher place. Examples are a ramp, a wedge, and a screw. **(C59)**

inertia—the tendency of all objects to stay still if they are still or to keep moving if they are moving. There is only a change in motion when an outside net force acts on the object. **(C44)**

lever—a simple machine made up of a board or bar that moves about a fulcrum. The pulley and the wheel and axle are examples of levers in other forms. **(C53)**

▲ A seesaw is a lever.

machine—a tool that changes either the amount of force acting on an object or the direction of the force. **(C53)**

magnetism—the force that magnets produce. Magnets pull on objects that are made of certain materials—usually iron or steel. Magnets also pull or push other magnets. **(C18)**

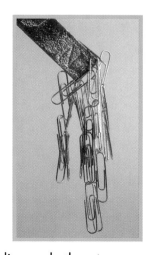

Magnets attract paper clips and other ▲ things made of iron or steel.

mass—the measure of the amount of matter in an object. Mass is measured in grams and kilograms with a pan balance. **(C15)**

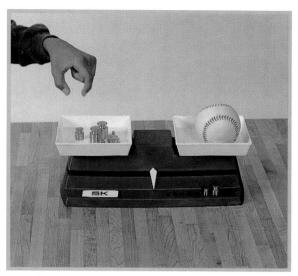

▲ All objects have mass.

simple machine—a machine with few or no moving parts. Levers and inclined planes are simple machines. **(C53)**

weight—the measure of the force of gravity on an object. Weight and other forces are measured with a spring scale in units called *newtons*. **(C27)**

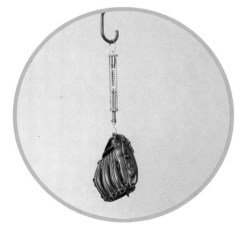

▲ The weight of objects can be measured.

REFERENCE HANDBOOK

Safety in the Classroom

Doing activities in science can be fun, but you need to be sure you do them safely. It is up to you, your teacher, and your classmates to make your classroom a safe place for science activities.

Think about what causes most accidents in everyday life—being careless, not paying attention, and showing off. The same kinds of behavior cause accidents in the science classroom.

Here are some ways to make your classroom a safe place.

WATCH YOUR EYES.
Wear safety goggles anytime you are directed to do so. If you should ever get any substance in your eyes, tell your teacher right away.

THINK AHEAD.
Study the steps of the activity so you know what to expect. If you have any questions about the steps, ask your teacher to explain. Be sure you understand any safety symbols that are shown in the activity.

BE NEAT.
Keep your work area clean. If you have long hair, pull it back so it doesn't get in the way. If you have long sleeves, roll them or push them up to keep them away from your experiment.

YUCK!
Never eat or drink anything during a science activity unless you are told to do so by your teacher.

OOPS!
If you should have an accident that causes a spill or breaks something, or if you get cut, tell your teacher right away.

DON'T GET SHOCKED.
Sometimes you need to use electric appliances, such as lamps, in an activity. You always need to be careful around electricity. Be sure that electric cords are in a safe place where you can't trip over them. Don't ever pull a plug out of an outlet by pulling on the cord.

KEEP IT CLEAN.
Always clean up when you have finished your activity. Put everything away and wipe your work area. Last of all, wash your hands.

Safety Symbols

In some activities, you will see a symbol that stands for what you need to do to stay safe. Do what the symbol stands for.

 This is a general symbol that tells you to be careful. Reading the steps of the activity will tell you exactly what you need to do to be safe.

 You will need to protect your eyes if you see this symbol. Put on safety goggles and leave them on for the entire activity.

 This symbol tells you that you will be using something sharp in the activity. Be careful not to cut or poke yourself or others.

 This symbol tells you something hot will be used in the activity. Be careful not to get burned or to cause someone else to get burned.

 This symbol tells you to put on an apron to protect your clothing.

 Don't touch! This symbol tells you that you will need to touch something that is hot. Use a thermal mitt to protect your hand.

 This symbol tells you that you will be using electric equipment. Use proper safety procedures.

Using a Hand Lens

A hand lens magnifies objects, or makes them look larger than they are.

▲ **This object is not in focus.**

Sometimes objects are too small for you to see easily without some help. You might want to see details that you cannot see with your eyes alone. When this happens, you can use a hand lens.

To use a hand lens, first place the object you want to look at on a flat surface, such as a table. Next, hold the hand lens over the object. At first, the object may appear blurry, like the object in **A**. Move the hand lens toward or away from the object until the object comes into sharp focus, as shown in **B**.

▲ **This object is focused clearly.**

Making a Water-Drop Lens

There may be times when you want to use a hand lens but there isn't one around. If that happens, you can make a water-drop lens to help you in the same way a hand lens does. A water-drop lens is best used to make flat objects, such as pieces of paper and leaves, seem larger.

MATERIALS
- sheet of acetate
- 2 rectangular rubber erasers
- water
- dropper

DO THIS

❶ Place the object to be magnified on a table between two identical erasers.

❷ Place a sheet of acetate on top of the erasers so that the sheet of acetate is about 1 cm above the object.

❸ Use the dropper to place one drop of water on the surface of the sheet over the object. Don't make the drop too large or it will make things look bent.

A water-drop lens can magnify objects. ▶

Caring For and Using a Microscope

A microscope, like a hand lens, magnifies objects. However, a microscope can increase the detail you see by increasing the number of times an object is magnified.

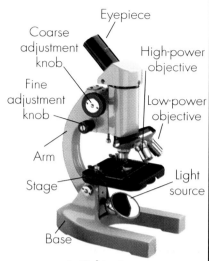

▲ **Light microscope**

(Eyepiece, Coarse adjustment knob, Fine adjustment knob, High-power objective, Low-power objective, Arm, Stage, Light source, Base)

CARING FOR A MICROSCOPE

- Always use two hands when you carry a microscope.
- Never touch any of the lenses of the microscope with your fingers.

USING A MICROSCOPE

1. Raise the eyepiece as far as you can using the coarse-adjustment knob. Place the slide you wish to view on the stage.

2. Always start by using the lowest power. The lowest-power lens is usually the shortest. Start with the lens in the lowest position it can go without touching the slide.

3. Look through the eyepiece and begin adjusting the eyepiece upward with the coarse-adjustment knob. When the slide is close to being in focus, use the fine-adjustment knob.

4. When you want to use the higher-power lens, first focus the slide under low power. Then, watching carefully to make sure that the lens will not hit the slide, turn the higher-power lens into place. Use only the fine-adjustment knob when looking through the higher-power lens.

Some of you may use a Brock microscope. This is a sturdy microscope that has only one lens.

1. Place the object to be viewed on the stage. Move the long tube, containing the lens, close to the stage.

2. Put your eye on the eyepiece, and begin raising the tube until the object comes into focus.

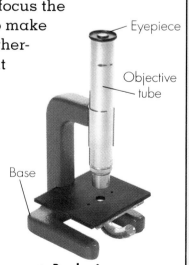

▲ **Brock microscope**

(Eyepiece, Objective tube, Base)

Using a Dropper

Use a dropper when you need to add small amounts of a liquid to another material.

A dropper has two main parts. One is a large empty part called a *bulb*. You hold the bulb and squeeze it to use the dropper. The other part of a dropper is long and narrow and is called a *tube*.

DO THIS

1 Use a clean dropper for each liquid you measure.

2 With the dropper out of the liquid, squeeze the bulb and keep it squeezed. Then dip the end of the tube into the liquid.

3 Release the pressure on the bulb. As you do so, you will see the liquid enter the tube.

▲ Using a dropper correctly

4 Take the dropper from the liquid, and move it to the place you want to put the liquid. If you are putting the liquid into another liquid, do not let the dropper touch the surface of the second liquid.

5 Gently squeeze the bulb until one drop comes out of the tube. Repeat slowly until you have measured out the right number of drops.

▲ Using a dropper incorrectly

Measuring Liquids

Use a beaker, a measuring cup, or a graduated cylinder to measure liquids accurately.

Containers for measuring liquids are made of clear or translucent materials so that you can see the liquid inside them. On the outside of each of these measuring tools, you will see lines and numbers that make up a scale. On most of the containers used by scientists, the scale is in milliliters (mL).

DO THIS

1 Pour the liquid you want to measure into one of the measuring containers. Make sure your measuring container is on a flat, stable surface, with the measuring scale facing you.

2 Look at the liquid through the container. Move so that your eyes are even with the surface of the liquid in the container.

3 To read the volume of the liquid, find the scale line that is even with the top of the liquid. In narrow containers, the surface of the liquid may look curved. Take your reading at the lowest point of the curve.

4 Sometimes the surface of the liquid may not be exactly even with a line. In that case, you will need to estimate the volume of the liquid. Decide which line the liquid is closer to, and use that number.

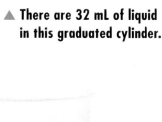

▲ There are 32 mL of liquid in this graduated cylinder.

▲ There are 27 mL of liquid in this beaker.

Using a Thermometer

Determine temperature readings of the air and most liquids by using a thermometer with a standard scale.

Most thermometers are thin tubes of glass that are filled with a red or silver liquid. As the temperature goes up, the liquid in the tube rises. As the temperature goes down, the liquid sinks. The tube is marked with lines and numbers that provide a temperature scale in degrees. Scientists use the Celsius scale to measure temperature. A temperature reading of 27 degrees Celsius is written 27°C.

DO THIS

1 Place the thermometer in the liquid whose temperature you want to record, but don't rest the bulb of the thermometer on the bottom or side of the container. If you are measuring the temperature of the air, make sure that the thermometer is not in direct sunlight or in line with a direct light source.

2 Move so that your eyes are e the liquid in the thermomete

3 If you are measuring a material that is not being heated or cooled, wait about two minutes for the reading to become stable. Find the scale line that meet the top of the liquid in the thermometer, and read the temperature.

4 If the material you are measuring is being heated o cooled, you will not be able t wait before taking your measurements. Measure as quickly as you can.

The temperature of this liquid is 27°C. ▶

Making a Thermometer

If you don't have a thermometer, you can make a simple one easily. The simple thermometer won't give you an exact temperature reading, but you can use it to tell if the temperature is going up or going down.

DO THIS

1 Add colored water to the jar until it is nearly full.

2 Place the straw in the jar. Finish filling the jar with water, but leave about 1 cm of space at the top.

3 Lift the straw until 10 cm of it stick up out of the jar. Use the clay to seal the mouth of the jar.

4 Use the dropper to add colored water to the straw until the straw is at least half full.

5 On the straw, mark the level of the water. "S" stands for *start*.

6 To get an idea of how your thermometer works, place the jar in a bowl of ice. Wait several minutes, and then mark the new water level on the straw. This new water level should be marked C for *cold*.

7 Take the jar out of the bowl of ice, and let it return to room temperature. Next, place the jar in a bowl of warm water. Wait several minutes, and then mark the new water level on the straw. This level can be labeled W for *warm*.

▶ You can use a thermometer like this to decide if the temperature of a liquid or the air is going up or down.

Using a Balance

Use a balance to measure an object's mass. Mass is the amount of matter an object has.

Most balances look like the one shown. They have two pans. In one pan, you place the object you want to measure. In the other pan, you place standard masses. Standard masses are objects that have a known mass. Grams are the units used to measure mass for most scientific activities.

DO THIS

1 First, make certain the empty pans are balanced. They are in balance if the pointer is at the middle mark on the base. If the pointer is not at this mark, move the slider to the right or left. Your teacher will help if you cannot balance the pans.

◀ **These pans are balanced and ready to be used to find the mass of an object.**

2 Place the object you wish to measure in one pan. The pointer will move toward the pan without the object in it.

3 Add the standard masses to the other pan. As you add masses, you should see the pointer begin to move. When the pointer is at the middle mark again, the pans are balanced.

4 Add the numbers on the masses you used. The total is the mass of the object you measured.

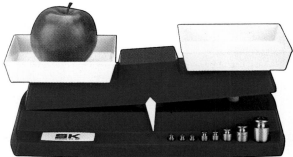

These pans are unbalanced. ▶

Making a Balance

If you do not have a balance, you can make one. A balance requires only a few simple materials. You can use nonstandard masses such as paper clips or nickels. This type of balance is best for measuring small masses.

DO THIS

1 If the ruler has holes in it, tie the string through the center hole. If it does not have holes, tie the string around the middle of the ruler.

2 Tape the other end of the string to a table. Allow the ruler to hang down from the side of the table. Adjust the ruler so that it is level.

3 Unbend the end of each paper clip slightly. Push these ends through the paper cups as shown. Attach each cup to the ruler by using the paper clips.

4 Adjust the cups until the ruler is level again.

MATERIALS
- 1 sturdy plastic or wooden ruler
- string
- transparent tape
- 2 paper cups
- 2 large paper clips

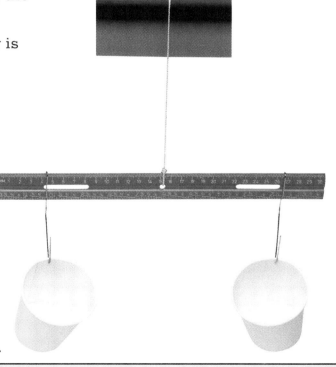

▶ **This balance is ready for use.**

Using a Spring Scale

A spring scale is a tool you use to measure the force of gravity on objects. You find the weight of the objects and use newtons as the unit of measurement for the force of gravity. You also use the spring scale and newtons to measure other forces.

A spring scale has two main parts. One part is a spring with a hook on the end. The hook is used to connect an object to the spring scale. The other part is a scale with numbers that tell you how many newtons of force are acting on the object.

DO THIS

With an Object at Rest

> With the object resting on the table, hook the spring scale to it. Do not stretch the spring at this point.
>
> Lift the scale and object with a smooth motion. Do not jerk them upward.
>
> Wait until any motion in the spring comes to a stop. Then read the number of newtons from the scale.

With an Object in Motion

> With the object resting on the table, hook the spring scale to it. Do not stretch the spring.
>
> Pull the object smoothly across the table. Do not jerk the object. If you pull with a jerky motion, the spring scale will wiggle too much for you to get a good reading.
>
> As you are pulling, read the number of newtons you are using to pull the object.

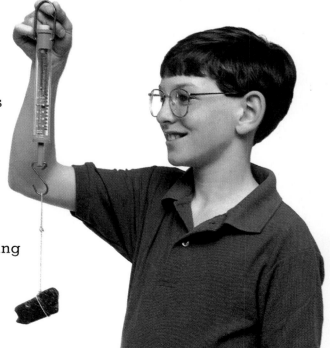

Making a Spring Scale

If you do not have a spring scale, you can make one by following the directions below.

DO THIS

1 Staple one end of the rubber band (the part with the sharp curve) to the middle of one end of the cardboard so that the rubber band hangs down the length of the cardboard. Color the loose end of the rubber band with a marker to make it easy to see.

2 Bend the paper clip so that it is slightly open and forms a hook. Hang the paper clip by its unopened end from the rubber band.

3 Put the narrow paper strip across the rubber band, and staple the strip to the cardboard. The rubber band and hook must be able to move easily.

4 While holding the cardboard upright, hang one 100-g mass from the hook. Allow the mass to come to rest, and mark the position of the bottom of the rubber band on the cardboard. Label this position on the cardboard 1 N. Add another 100-g mass for a total of 200 g.

5 Continue to add masses and mark the cardboard. Each 100-g mass adds a force of about 1 N.

MATERIALS

- heavy cardboard (10cm x 30cm)
- large rubber band
- stapler
- marker
- large paper clip
- paper strip (about 1 cm x 3 cm)
- 100-g masses (about 1 N each)

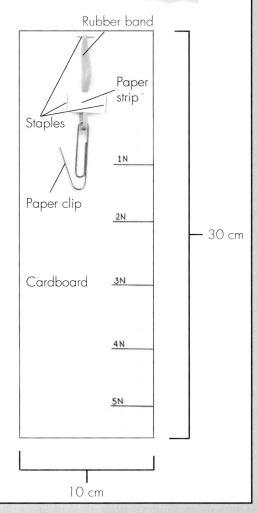

Rubber band
Paper strip
Staples
Paper clip
Cardboard

1N
2N
3N
4N
5N

30 cm

10 cm

Working Like a Scientist
What Do Rabbits Like to Eat?

Have you ever wanted to know about something but you didn't know how to find out about it? Working like a scientist can help. Read the story below to find out how Alita, Juan, and Jasmine learned to work like scientists.

Alita, Juan, and Jasmine were friends. Each of them owned a rabbit. "I'd like to give my rabbit a treat," Alita told Juan and Jasmine. "I want the treat to be something that my rabbit likes. It should also be good for the rabbit."

"What do you think the best treat would be?" Juan asked.

"That's a good question," Jasmine said. "How can we find out the answer?"

Asking a good question is the first step in working like a scientist. A good question helps you find out what the problem is. A good question starts you on the way to finding an answer. Often a good question will have many answers.

DO THIS

Ask a question.
Form a hypothesis.
Design a test. Do the test.
Record what happened.
Draw a conclusion.

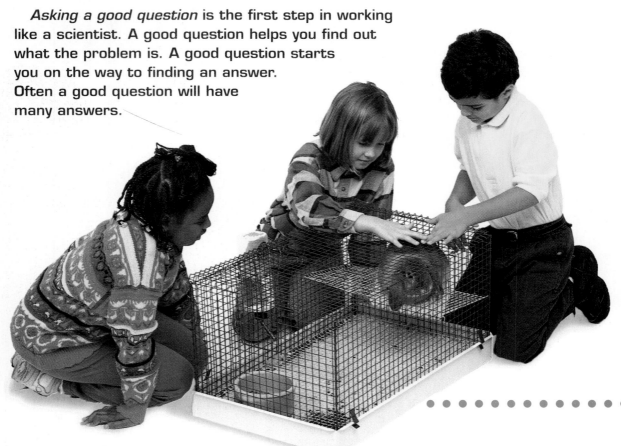

After you ask a good question, you need to choose one possible answer and then find out if your answer is right. This possible answer to your question is called a *hypothesis*. You *form a hypothesis* when you choose an answer to a question. Sometimes you must do research before you can choose an answer. Find out how Alita, Juan, and Jasmine formed their hypothesis.

DO THIS

Ask a question.

Form a hypothesis.

Design a test. Do the test.

Record what happened.

Draw a conclusion.

The next day, Alita, Juan, and Jasmine met at Alita's house. Juan and Jasmine had brought their rabbits in their carrying cages.

"We need to find out what the best treat for a rabbit would be," Juan said.

Alita said, "My grandpa told me that rabbits like all kinds of vegetables. Maybe vegetables would be the best treat."

"I gave my rabbit some celery once and she didn't eat it at all. I wonder if my rabbit is different," Juan replied.

Jasmine said, "Why don't we say that we think rabbits like carrots, celery, and broccoli? Then we could test our rabbits to see if we're right."

"Yes," Alita said. "We can offer each rabbit carrots, celery, and broccoli and see what each one likes best."

"That sounds like a good idea," Juan said.

When Jasmine said to *do a test*, she was talking about doing an experiment. An experiment must be carefully designed and planned. You must decide how to do your test and how to record the results.

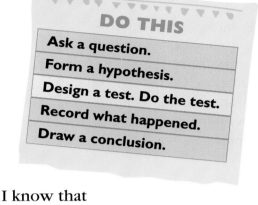

DO THIS

Ask a question.

Form a hypothesis.

Design a test. Do the test.

Record what happened.

Draw a conclusion.

Alita said, "We can put the three kinds of vegetables in each cage. We can watch our rabbits and see which vegetables they eat."

Jasmine said, "But we should do the test when we know our rabbits aren't very hungry. If they were, they might eat anything. I know that when I'm very hungry, I eat anything."

"That's true," Juan said. "And we shouldn't put one vegetable closer to the rabbit than the other vegetables. The rabbit might eat the first vegetable it saw. It might not eat the vegetable it liked best."

Alita said, "That sounds good. Let me write that down."

Jasmine said, "I've been thinking about our test. How are we going to know what the answer is? We should be able to say why we're giving our rabbits a certain kind of treat."

Juan said, "That's a good question. We have to find a way to record what our rabbits do."

Alita smiled. She showed Juan and Jasmine a chart.

"I made up this chart. It has a place for each rabbit and each kind of vegetable. We can see which vegetable each rabbit eats first."

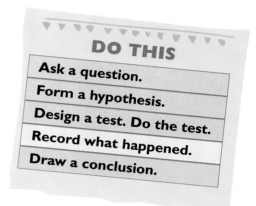

DO THIS

Ask a question.

Form a hypothesis.

Design a test. Do the test.

Record what happened.

Draw a conclusion.

A Rabbit's Favorite Treat									
	Broccoli			Carrots			Celery		
	1st	2nd	3rd	1st	2nd	3rd	1st	2nd	3rd
Jasmine's Rabbit									
Juan's Rabbit									
Alita's Rabbit									

What Alita showed Juan and Jasmine was a way to record what they saw the rabbits do. This is called *recording data.* It is an important part of science because it helps you explain why you think one answer may be right and another may be wrong.

Alita, Juan, and Jasmine put broccoli, carrots, and celery into the three rabbit cages. Alita's rabbit smelled the broccoli and then hopped to the carrots.

The rabbit ate some of the carrots, but it did not eat the celery. Jasmine's rabbit ate the carrots and a little bit of the celery. Juan's rabbit ate only the carrots.

Alita filled in the chart, and the three friends looked at it. Jasmine said, "It looks as if all three rabbits like carrots. My rabbit likes celery. None of the rabbits like broccoli."

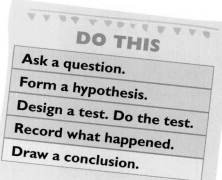

DO THIS

Ask a question.
Form a hypothesis.
Design a test. Do the test.
Record what happened.
Draw a conclusion.

A Rabbit's Favorite Treat	Broccoli			Carrots			Celery		
	1st	2nd	3rd	1st	2nd	3rd	1st	2nd	3rd
Jasmine's Rabbit				X				X	
Juan's Rabbit				X					
Alita's Rabbit				X					

What Jasmine did is *draw a conclusion*. She looked at the results of the test and was able to say what she thought the test showed. Just doing a test is not enough. You must be able to say what the test showed you.

"We haven't tried all vegetables," Juan said.

"No," Alita said. "And we didn't measure how much of the carrots and celery Jasmine's rabbit ate."

"We can do more tests," Jasmine said.

"All right," Alita said. "That would be fun!"

Juan said, "But for now, we know that our rabbits like carrots. So we can give them carrots for treats."

INDEX

Note: Page numbers in italics indicate illustrations.

Axis, Earth's, *B19*, B78
Axle, *C56*
> See *also* Wheels and axles

Baboons, *A56*
Backbone
> activity, A44
> animals with, *A43*–A47
> animals without, A48–A49
Bacteria, *D61*
Baden-Powell, B. F. S., E46–E47
Balance, *C15, C79, R10, R11*
Balancing (Jennings), C9
Ballonets (blimp), *E36*–*E37*
Ballonet valves, *E36*–*E37*
Balloon, *B43, B46, E12*
> weight of air in, B43
> See *also* Hot-air balloon; Weather balloon
Bare, Colleen Stanley, A9
Bar magnets, *C20*–*C21*
Barometer, *B46, B47, B48, B49, B50, B51, B52, B53*
> activities, B46–B47, B52–B53
> defined, B78
> development of, B48–B51
> kinds of, B51
> uses of, B48
Basket (hot-air balloon), *E32*
Beagle, *A13*
Beaker, *R7*
Beaks
> activity, A26–A27
> of birds, A26–A27, *A29*
> of a falcon, *A47*
Beams, Bill, *B55*–*B57*
Bear, *A66*
Beavers, A15, *D42*
Bengal tiger, *A24*
Bernoulli, Daniel, E23
Biplanes, *E2*–*E3*
Birds, *A3, A12, A15, A29, A36, A43, A54, A94*

beaks of, A26–A27, *A29*, A47
behavior of, A54
camouflage of, A94
classifying, A40, *A43, A45*, A47
eggs of, A79
feathers of, A17
in freshwater ecosystem, D18, D42, D46
migration of, A60–A64
nesting of, A15
spine of, A43
Bison, A70, *A71, B3*
Bjork, Christina, B9
Blimps, E26, E34–E37, *E35*, *E36*–*E37*
> parts of, E36–E37
> uses of, E35
Bluegills, *D14*
Blue heron, *D18*
Boa constrictor, *A74*
Body coverings, A16–A20, *A16, A17, A20*
Bogong moths, *A95*
Boring, Mel, C68–C71
Botswana, *D28*–*D29*
Bottle opener, *C54*
Brain, effects of pollution on, B67
Breathing, A14–A15
Bridges, C3, C6, *C30*–*C33*
> activity, C72–C73
> types of, C30–C33
Bridges (Robbins), C9
Bridge That Couldn't Be Built, The (Boring), C68–C71
Brook, *D54*
Brooklyn Bridge (NY), *C3*
Brown, Ken, E8
Bucket wheel excavator, *C65*
Bullfrog, *D29*
Burner (hot-air balloon), *E32, E33*
Buson, E18
Busy Busy Squirrels (Bare), A9
Butterfly
> from egg, *A88*–*A89*
> migration of, *A60*

Cable, C57
CALTRANS, C66
Camel, *A32*
Camouflage, A23, A24, A94
> as defense, A23–A24
> defined, A23, A94
Camp Springs (MD), B56
Canada, *B25*
Canada geese, activity, A62–A63
Canadian musk oxen, *A56*
Canis familiaris, A42
Can opener, *C23, C64, C78*
Can Rain Be Dangerous?, B69–B73
Cantilever bridge, *C33*
Carapace, *A34*
Careers
> bird sanctuary worker, *A64*
> environmentalist, D72–D73
> heavy-equipment operator, C66–C67
> meteorologist, E70–E71
> weather reporter, B6
> weather researcher, B7
> weather scientist, B55–B57
Carolina Sandhills National Wildlife Refuge, A62–A63
Carter, Gale, E70–E71
Cartoon (*Calvin and Hobbes*), x
Cat, *A80*–*A83*
Catfish, *D15*
Celsius temperature, R8
Chandra, Deborah, E19
Chemicals, as pollutants, *B60, B70*
Cherry, Lynne, D9
Chicken, *A75, A79*
Cirrus clouds, *B33, B78*
Clam, *A49*
Clarke, Barry, D9
Classifying, A10, A39, A85
> reasons for, A37
> scientific, A40–A41

ACKNOWLEDGMENTS

For permission to reprint copyrighted material, grateful acknowledgment is made to the following sources:

Mel Boring: From "The Bridge That Couldn't Be Built" in *Cricket* Magazine, June 1991. Text © by Mel Boring.

Carolrhoda Books, Inc., Minneapolis, MN: Cover illustration from *How the Guinea Fowl Got Her Spots* by Barbara Knutson. Copyright © 1990 by Barbara Knutson.

Children's Better Health Institute, Indianapolis, IN: From "Magic Jumpson" (originally titled "The Froggie") in *Jack and Jill* Magazine, March 1991. Text copyright © 1988 by Children's Better Health Institute, Benjamin Franklin Literary & Medical Society, Inc.

Coward, McCann & Geoghegan: Abridged from "Amelia Earhart" by Peggy Mann in *Amelia Earhart, First Lady of Flight.* Text copyright © 1970 by Peggy Mann.

Current Health 1® Magazine: "Can Rain Be Dangerous?" from *Current Health 1®* Magazine, November 1991. Text copyright © 1991 by Weekly Reader Corporation. Published by Weekly Reader Corporation.

Dial Books for Young Readers, a division of Penguin Books USA Inc.: Cover illustration from *Bridges* by Ken Robbins. Copyright © 1991 by Ken Robbins.

Doubleday, a division of Bantam Doubleday Dell Publishing Group, Inc.: Cover illustration from *Why Can't I Fly?* by Ken Brown. Copyright © 1990 by Ken Brown.

Dutton Children's Books, a division of Penguin Books USA Inc.: From *It's an Armadillo!* by Bianca Lavies. Copyright © 1989 by Bianca Lavies.

Farrar, Straus & Giroux, Inc.: "Ribbons of Wind" from *Balloons and Other Poems* by Deborah Chandra. Text copyright © 1988, 1990 by Deborah Chandra.

Frank Fretz: Illustration by Frank Fretz from "Only the Tough Survive" by James Halfpenny in *Ranger Rick* Magazine, December 1993.

Harcourt Brace & Company: Cover illustration from *A River Ran Wild* by Lynne Cherry. Copyright © 1992 by Lynne Cherry.

The Hokuseido Press, Tokyo, Japan: Untitled haiku (Retitled: "Japanese Poem") by Buson from *Haiku,* Vols. 1-4, translated by R. H. Blyth.

Holiday House, Inc.: Cover illustration from *Weather Words and What They Mean* by Gail Gibbons. Copyright © 1990 by Gail Gibbons.

Richard Lewis: Untitled poem (Retitled: "African Bushman Poem") from *Out of the Earth I Sing,* edited by Richard Lewis. Text copyright © 1968 by Richard Lewis.

Little, Brown and Company: From *Four Corners of the Sky: Poems, Chants and Oratory* (Retitled: "Native American Kiowa Verse"), selected by Theodore Clymer. Text copyright © 1975 by Theodore Clymer.

Little, Brown and Company, in Association with Arcade Publishing, Inc.: Cover illustration by Ted Rand from *Water's Way* by Lisa Westberg Peters. Illustration copyright © 1991 by Ted Rand.

Lothrop, Lee & Shepard Books, a division of William Morrow & Company, Inc.: Cover illustration by Catherine Stock from *Galimoto* by Karen Lynn Williams. Illustration copyright © 1990 by Catherine Stock.

National Wildlife Federation: "Amazing Jumping Machine" by Carolyn Duckworth from *Ranger Rick* Magazine, March 1991. Text copyright 1991 by the National Wildlife Federation. "Only the Tough Survive" by James Halfpenny from *Ranger Rick* Magazine, December 1993. Text copyright 1993 by the National Wildlife Federation. Drawings by Jack Shepherd from "Magic Jumpson" in *Ranger Rick* Magazine, March 1991. Copyright 1991 by the National Wildlife Federation.

North-South Books Inc., New York: Cover illustration from *The Air Around Us* by Eleonore Schmid. Copyright © 1992 by Nord-Sud Verlag AG, Gossau Zürich, Switzerland.

Marian Reiner: Untitled haiku (Retitled: "Japanese Poem") by Asayasu from *More Cricket Songs,* translated by Harry Behn. Text copyright © 1971 by Harry Behn.

Sierra Club Books for Children: From *Come Back, Salmon* by Molly Cone. Text copyright © 1992 by Molly Cone.

Simon & Schuster Books for Young Readers, New York: Cover illustration from *Frog Odyssey* by Juliet and Charles Snape. © 1991 by Juliet and Charles Snape.

Gareth Stevens, Inc., Milwaukee, WI: From *Rockets, Probes, and Satellites* by Isaac Asimov. © 1988 by Nightfall, Inc.

Walker and Company: Cover illustration by Valerie A. Kells from *One Earth, a Multitude of Creatures* by Peter and Connie Roop. Illustration copyright © 1992 by Valerie A. Kells.

PHOTO CREDITS

Key: (t)top, (b)bottom, (l)left, (r)right, (c)center, (bg)background.

Front Cover, All Other Photographs: (tl), Robert Maier/Animals Animals; (tr), NASA/International Stock Photo; (c), Jean-Francois Causse/Tony Stone Images; (cr), Kristian Hilsen/Tony Stone Images; (bl), Benn Mitchell/The Image Bank; (br), E.R. Degginger/Color-Pic.

Back Cover, Harcourt Brace & Company Photographs: (t), Greg Leary; (bl), Earl Kogler.

Back Cover, All Other Photographs: (br), Kaz Mori/The Image Bank.

To The Student, Harcourt Brace & Company Photographs: vi(tr), vi(c), Weronica Ankarorn; vi(b), Maria Paraskevas; viii, Earl Kogler; xv(b), Jerry White.

To The Student, All Other Photographs: iv(tl), Neena Wilmot/Stock/Art Images; iv(tr), Jane Burton/Bruce Coleman, Inc.; iv(bl), Dwight R. Kuhn; iv(br), Dave B. Fleetham/Tom Stack & Assoc.; v(t), Dave Bartruff; v(b), Photri; vi(tl), W. Hille/Leo de Wys, Inc.; vii(l), Stephen Dalton/Photo Researchers; vii(r), John Gerlach/Tom Stack & Assoc.; x, David Young-Wolff/PhotoEdit; xi(t), T. Rosenthal/SuperStock; xi(b), Gabe Palmer/The Stock Market; xii, Myrleen Ferguson Cate/PhotoEdit; xiii, Tony Freeman/PhotoEdit; xiv(l), Jeff Greenberg/Photo Researchers; xiv(r), Russell D. Curtis/Photo Researchers; xv(t), Bob Daemmrich; xvi(l), Myrleen Ferguson Cate/PhotoEdit; xvi(r), Bob Daemmrich/Stock, Boston.

Unit A, Harcourt Brace & Company Photographs: A4-A5, A6(t), A7, Dick Krueger; A8, A9, Weronica Ankarorn; A10-A11, Dick Krueger; A16(r), A17(tr), A17(b), A19, A20(b), A22, A27, A37, A38, A43(l), A44, Earl Kogler; A63, Eric Camden; A76, A86, Earl Kogler; A92-A93(bg), David Lavine; A92(t), A93, Earl Kogler.

Unit A, All Other Photographs: Unit Page Divider, Erwin & Peggy Bauer; A1, A2-A3, Alan & Sandy Carey; A3, Hugh P. Smith, Jr.; A6(b), Alan Briere/SuperStock; A12(bg), Index Stock; A12(t), David R. Frazier; A12(b), William Johnson/Stock, Boston; A13(t), Henry Ausloos/Animals Animals; A13(b), Antoinette

Jongen/SuperStock; A14(t), John Cancalosi/Stock, Boston; A14(b), M. Bruce/SuperStock; A15(t), Stephen G. Maka/Lightwave; A15(b), H. Lanks/SuperStock; A16(l), G. Corbett/SuperStock; A17(tl), Stephen J. Krasemann/NHPA; A20(t), M. Burgess/SuperStock; A21, A. Mercieca/SuperStock; A23(t), Dwight R. Kuhn; A23(b), James T. Jones/David R. Frazier Photolibrary; A24(t), SuperStock; A24(b), Stephen G. Maka/Lightwave; A25(t), Gary Bell/The Wildlife Collection; A25(cl), Larry A. Brazil; A25(cr), Stephen J. Krasemann/Valan Photos; A25(b), David Cavagnaro/Peter Arnold, Inc.; A28, The Granger Collection; A30(tl), A. Kaiser/SuperStock; A30(tr), Stephen Dalton/NHPA; A30(b), Aaron Haupt/David R. Frazier Photolibrary; A31, A32(t), SuperStock; A32(c), John Giustina/The Wildlife Collection; A32(b), Sven-Olaf Lindblad/Photo Researchers; A33(t), A33(b), A34(t), A34(c), A34(b), A35(l), A35(r), Bianca Lavies; A36(bg), Rod Planck/Tony Stone Images; A36(t), Scot Stewart; A36(b), Stephen G. Maka/Lightwave; A39(tl), Bill Tronca/Tom Stack & Assoc.; A39(tc), A39(tr), T. Wolf Bolz/TexStockPhotoInc.; A39(bl), David M. Dennis/Tom Stack & Assoc.; A39(bc), Claudio Ferer/Devaney Stock Photos; A39(br), Gerald & Buff Corsi/Tom Stack & Assoc.; A40, Leonard Lee Rue III/Animals Animals; A41, Tetsu Yamazaki; A42, Bob Daemmrich/The Image Works; A43(r), Don Enger/Animals Animals; A45(l), Ron & Valerie Taylor/Bruce Coleman, Inc.; A45(r), A46(t), Zig Leszczynski/Animals Animals; A46(cl), E.R. Degginger/Color-Pic; A46(cr), Renee Lynn/Photo Researchers; A46(b), Holton Collection/SuperStock; A47(tl), Alan G. Nelson/Animals Animals; A47(tr), E.R. Degginger/Animals Animals; A47(c), Fred Whitehead/Animals Animals; A47(b), Dominique Braud/Tom Stack & Assoc.; A48(t), Brian Parker/Tom Stack & Assoc.; A48(b), Oxford Scientific Films/Animals Animals; A49(tl), Dwight R. Kuhn; A49(tc), Lester V. Bergman & Assoc.; A49(tr), Rod Planck/Tom Stack & Assoc.; A49(cl), Biophoto Associates/Photo Researchers; A49(cr), John Shaw/Tom Stack & Assoc.; A49(b), Dave B. Fleetham/Tom Stack & Assoc.; A52(bg), Tim Fitzharris/Masterfile; A52(t) H. Morton/SuperStock; A52(b), John Cancalosi/Valan Photos; A53, D. Robert Franz/The Wildlife Collection; A54(tl), Stephen G. Maka/Lightwave; A54(tr), Hank Andrews/Visuals Unlimited; A54(b), Mike Bacon/Tom Stack & Assoc.; A55(t), Stephen G. Maka/Lightwave; A55(b), SuperStock; A56(t), Stephen G. Maka/Lightwave; A56(c), Gerald & Buff Corsi/Tom Stack & Assoc.; A56(b), Fred Bruemmer/Valan Photos; A57(t), Scot Stewart; A57(b), Western History Department/Denver Public Library; A58(tl), A58(tr), Daniel W. Gotshall; A58(bl) SuperStock; A58(br), Dwight R. Kuhn; A59(t), SuperStock; A59(b), John Cancalosi/Valan Photos; A61(t), M. Bruce/SuperStock; A61(b), SuperStock; A62-A63(bg), Index Stock; A64(t) A64(b) Master's Studio; A65, Jane Burton/Bruce Coleman, Inc.; A66, Mark Sherman/Bruce Coleman, Inc.; A67, Michael S. Quinton; A68(t), Erwin & Peggy Bauer; A68(bl), Frank Fretz; A68(br), Erwin & Peggy Bauer; A69, Stephen J. Krasemann/DRK; A70, Leonard Lee Rue III; A71, Erwin & Peggy Bauer; A72(bg), Gregory Dimijian/Photo Researchers; A72(t), John Colwell/Grant Heilman Photography; A72(b), H. Mark Weidman; A73, David R. Frazier; A74(t), Allen Russell/ProFiles West; A74(c), Doug Perrine/Innerspace Visions; A74(b), John Cancalosi/Tom Stack & Assoc.; A75(t), John Fowler/Valan Photos; A75(cl), Dwight R. Kuhn; A75(cr), Stephen G. Maka/Lightwave; A75(b), Martin Harvey/The Wildlife Collection; A77, Wolfgang Kaehler; A78(t), Dr. Paul V. Loiselle; A78(b), John T. Pennington/Ivy Images; A79, Martin Harvey/The Wildlife Collection; A80, A81(t), A81(b), A82(t), A82(cl), A82(cr), A82(b), A83(t), Dwight R. Kuhn; A83(bl), A83(br), Renee Stockdale/Animals Animals; A84(tl), Dwight R. Kuhn; A84(tr), Tom & Pat Leeson/DRK; A84(bl), Mella Panzella/Animals Animals; A84(br), Neena Wilmot/Stock/Art Images; A85(tl), Gary Braasch; A85(tr), Brian Parker/Tom Stack & Assoc.; A85(cl), A85(c), SuperStock; A85(cr), Gary Braasch; A85(b), A88(t), A88(cl), A88(cr), A88(b), A89(l), A89(r), Dwight R. Kuhn; A90-A91, Index Stock; A91(l), SuperStock; A91(r), A. Briere/SuperStock; A92(b), Allen Russell/ProFiles West; A94(t), Sven-Olaf Lindblad/Photo Researchers; A94(c), Anthony J. Bond/Valan Photos; A94(b), Stephen J. Krasemann/Valan Photos; A95(l), Wolfgang Bayer/Bruce Coleman, Inc.; A95(r), A. Mercieca/SuperStock.

Unit B, Harcourt Brace & Company Photographs: B4-B5, B6(t), B7(t), B7(b), Dick Krueger; B8, B9, Weronica Ankarorn; B10-B11, Maria Paraskevas; B14, B15, B16, B17, B20, Earl Kogler; B23(cb), Rodney Jones; B28(bc), B29(t), B29(b), B30, B36, B37, Earl Kogler; B40(bg), David Phillips; B41, B42, Earl Kogler; B43, Richard Nowitz; B44, B46(t), B46(b), B47, B53, Earl Kogler; B55(t), B55(b), B56(l), B56(r), B57, Jerry Heasley; B61, B63, B68, Richard T. Nowitz; B76(t), B76(b), Earl Kogler; B77(b), Richard T. Nowitz; 79(t), Earl Kogler.

Unit B, All Other Photographs: Unit Page Divider, A. Farquhar/Valan Photos; B1, Amy Drutman; B2-3, Gordon Wiltsie/Peter Arnold, Inc.; B3, Alan & Sandy Carey; B6(c), R. Dahlquist/SuperStock; B6(b), George Cargill/Lightwave; B12(bg), Jay Maisel; B12, Scott Barrow; B18(l), B18(r), B19(l), B19(r), E.R. Degginger/Bruce Coleman, Inc.; B22(t), SuperStock; B22(ct), David R. Frazier; B22(cb), Scott Barrow; B22(b), Hans & Judy Beste/Earth Scenes; B23(t), Scott Barrow; B23(ct), Harry M. Walker; B23(b), Loren McIntyre; B24(tl), Will & Deni McIntyre/AllStock; B24(tr), Tony Freeman/PhotoEdit; B24(cl), J.C. Carton/Bruce Coleman, Inc.; B24(cr), Richard T. Nowitz; B24(b), Fotoconcept; B25(t), John Eastcott, Yva Momatiuk/Valan Photos; B25(b), Sovfoto; B27, David Falconer/David R. Frazier Photolibrary; B28(bg), Dwight R. Kuhn; B28(t), Steve Solum/Bruce Coleman, Inc.; B28(bl), David R. Frazier; B28(br), Dave Bartruff; B32-B33, Gary Black/Masterfile; B32, Peter Griffith/Masterfile; B33, Mark Tomalty/Masterfile; B34, Peter Miller/Photo Researchers; B35(t), Alan Hicks/AllStock; B35(c), Wouterloot-Gregoire/Valan Photos; B35(b), Joyce Photographics/Valan Photos; B36-B37(bg), Dick Thomas/Visuals Unlimited; B40(t), Phil Degginger/Color-Pic; B40(b), Tony Freeman/PhotoEdit; B48, The Granger Collection; B50(bg), John Running/Stock, Boston; B50, The Granger Collection; B51(t) David R. Frazier; B51(b), Photri; B52, Runk, Schoenberger/Grant Heilman Photography; B54(l), A. Farquhar/Valan Photos; B54(r), SuperStock; B58(bg), David Woodfall/Tony Stone Images; B58(t), E.R. Degginger/Color-Pic; B58(b), Jose L. Pelaez/The Stock Market; B59, R. Llewellyn/SuperStock; B60(t), E.R. Degginger/Color-Pic; B60(c), Tony Freeman/PhotoEdit; B60(b), Anna Zuckerman/PhotoEdit; B62-B63(bg), E.R. Degginger/Color-Pic; B64, B65, B66, David R. Frazier; B67, Tony Freeman/PhotoEdit; B69, Ruth Dixon; B70, North Wind; B71, Phil Degginger/Color-Pic; B72(t), Bill Weedmark; B72(b), Dave Bartruff; B73, Grapes Michaud/Photo Researchers; B74-B75, J.R. Page/Valan Photos; B75(t), Valerie Wilkinson/Valan Photos; B75(b), SuperStock; B76-B77(bg), Greg Vaughn/Tom Stack & Assoc.; B77(t), Aaron Haupt/David R. Frazier Photolibrary; B78(t), Runk, Schoenberger/Grant Heilman Photography; B78(b), Mark Tomalty/Masterfile; B79(c) Gary Black/Masterfile; B79(b), John Heseltine/Photo Researchers; B80(l), Peter Griffith/Masterfile; B80(r), A. Upitis/SuperStock.

Unit C, Harcourt Brace & Company Photographs: C4-C5, C6(c), C6(b), C7(t), David Phillips; C7(c), Earl Kogler; C7(b), David Phillips; C8, C9, Weronica Ankarorn; C10-C11, C13, C14(b), C15(t), C15(bl), C15(br), C16, C17, C19(tl), C19(tr), C19(b), Earl Kogler; C20-C21(bg), Jerry White; C20, C21(t), C21(bl), C21(br),

C22(tr), C22(br), C23(tl), C23(c), C23(b), C24, C25, C28(l), C28(c), C28(r), C29(t), C29(b), Earl Kogler; C32(t), Gerald Ratto; C35, Earl Kogler; C36, C37, C39, C40, C43(t), C43(c), C43(b), C45(t), Dick Krueger; C45(b), Rob Downey; C46-C47(bg), Dick Krueger; C46, C47, Weronica Ankarorn; C48, Dick Krueger; C52(b), C53, Maria Paraskevas; C54(t), Bruce Wilson; C54(cl), Weronica Ankarorn; C54(cr), Earl Kogler; C54(b), Weronica Ankarorn; C55, Earl Kogler; C56(t), C56(b), C57(t), Maria Paraskevas; C58, Earl Kogler; C59(t), C59(b), Maria Paraskevas; C60, C61, C63(t), C63(b), C64, Earl Kogler; C66(t), C66(b), C67, Robert Landau; C73, C75(t), Earl Kogler; C75(b), David Phillips; C76(t), Earl Kogler; C76(b), David Phillips; C77, Jerry White; C78(l), Earl Kogler; C79(tl), Bruce Wilson; C79(tr), Earl Kogler; C79(bl), David Phillips; C79(br), Earl Kogler.

Unit C, All Other Photographs: Unit Page Divider, Bud Nielsen/ Lightwave; C1, Richard T. Nowitz/Valan Photos; C2-C3, David R. Frazier; C3, Rapho/Photo Researchers; C6(t), SuperStock; C12(bg), Harold Sund/The Image Bank; C12(t), James Blank/Zephyr Pictures; C12(b), W. Hille/Leo de Wys, Inc.; C14(t), Terry Wild Studio; C14(c), Ewing Galloway; C22(l), T. Matsumoto/Sygma; C23(tr), E.R. Degginger/Earth Scenes; C24-C25(bg), NASA; C26, The Bettmann Archive; C27, Lewis Portnoy/Spectra-Action; C30, Christopher Liu/ChinaStock; C31(t), Milt & Joan Mann/Cameramann; C31(b), Harry M. Walker; C32(b), Robert Frerck/Odyssey Productions; C33, Yves Tessier/Tessima; C34(bg), Roy Ooms/Masterfile; C34(t), John Terence Turner/FPG; C34(b), Alissa Crandall; C38-C39(bg), SuperStock; C41, Paul Souders/AllStock; C42(t), David R. Frazier; C42(c), C42(b), Alan & Sandy Carey; C44, NASA/Photri; C49, Dave Bartruff; C50-C51(bg), William Warren/West Light; C50(all), C51(all), Insurance Institute for Highway Safety; C52(bg), Index Stock; C52(t), Bud Nielsen/Lightwave; C57(b), Neena M. Wilmot/Stock/Art Images; C62(t), Ruth Dixon; C62(c), Dave Bartruff; C62(b), Aldo Mastrocola/Lightwave; C68, Steinman, Boynton, Gronquist & Birdsall; C70-C71, Frederic Stein/FPG; C72-C73(bg), Ken Graham; C74-C75(bg), SuperStock; C76-C77(bg), Andrew Sacks/Tony Stone Images; C78(r), Lewis Portony/Spectra-Action.

Unit D, Harcourt Brace & Company Photographs: D4-D5, Earl Kogler; D6(t), Dick Krueger; D8, D9, Weronica Ankarorn; D10-D11, D22, D23(b), Britt Runion; D24, Earl Kogler; D25, D26-D27, Britt Runion; D37(t), D37(b), D60(t), D62(t), D62(b) D63, D64, D65, Earl Kogler; D72, D73, Robert Landau; D76, D77(t), Richard T. Nowitz; D77(b), Earl Kogler.

Unit D, All Other Photographs: Unit Page Divider, Mark J. Thomas/Dembinsky Photo Assoc; D1, D2-D3, Larry Lefever/ Grant Heilman Photography; D3, Adam Jones/Dembinsky Photo Assoc.; D6(b), William McKinney/FPG; D7, Neena M. Wilmot/Stock/Art Images; D12(bg), Greg Nikas/Viesti Assoc.; D12(t), David R. Frazier; D12(b), Ruth Dixon; D13, Rod Planck/Tom Stack & Assoc.; D14(t), M.P.L. Fogden/Bruce Coleman, Inc.; D14(b), E.R. Degginger/Bruce Coleman, Inc.; D15(t), S. Maimone/SuperStock; D15(b), John Gerlach/Tom Stack & Assoc.; D16-D17(bg), Gabe Palmer/The Stock Market; D16, Gary Meszaros/Dembinsky Photo Assoc.; D17, John Shaw/Bruce Coleman, Inc.; D18(t), Mark J. Thomas/Dembinsky Photo Assoc.; D18(b), J.H. Robinson/Photo Researchers; D19, Gay Bumgarner/Photo Network; D23(t), Patti Murray/Earth Scenes; D28-D29, Betsy Blass/Photo Researchers; D29(tl), Karl H. Switak/Photo Researchers; D29(tr), E.R. Degginger/Color-Pic; D30(bg), Stephen G. Maka/Lightwave; D30(t), Stephen Dalton/Photo Researchers; D30(b), Stephen J. Krasemann/Valan Photos; D31, Stephen Dalton/Photo Researchers; D32(t), Zig Leszczynski/Animals Animals; D32(c), J.H. Robinson/Animals Animals; D32(b), Zig Leszczynski/Animals Animals; D33(t), Kim

Taylor/Bruce Coleman, Inc.; D33(b), Gregory Dimijian/Photo Researchers; D38(t), D38(b), D39(t), D39(c), D39(b), Dwight R. Kuhn; D44(bg), SuperStock; D44(t), P. Van Rhijn/SuperStock; D44(b), Bob & Clara Calhoun/Bruce Coleman, Inc.; D46, D47 Dwight R. Kuhn; D48(t), Mildred McPhee/Valan Photos; D48(cl), Bill Beatty/Wild & Natural; D48(cr), E.R. Degginger/Color-Pic; D48(cb), Glen D. Chambers; D48(bl), J. Faircloth/ Transparencies; D48(br), Oxford Scientific Films/Animals Animals; D49(t), J.A. Wilkinson/Valan Photos; D49(cl), Bill Beatty/Wild & Natural; D49(cr), Steve Maslowski/Valan Photos; D49(cb), Thomas Kitchin/Tom Stack & Assoc.; D49((bl), Bill Beatty/Wild & Natural; D49(br), John Shaw/Bruce Coleman, Inc.; D54, Phillip Norton/Valan Photos; D56-D57, Manley/SuperStock; D56, John Eastcott, Yva Momatiuk/Stock, Boston; D58(bg), R. Dahlquist/SuperStock; D58(t), M. Roessler/SuperStock; D58(b), D59, SuperStock; D60(b), Mark E. Gibson; D61(t), Dwight R. Kuhn; D61(b), A. Hennek/SuperStock; D66, D67(t), D67(b), D68, D69, D70(tl), D70(tr), D70(b), Sidnee Wheelwright; D71(t), Chris Huss/The Wildlife Collection; D71(c), D71(b), Sidnee Wheelwright; D74-D75(bg), SuperStock; D75, Nancy Sefton/Photo Researchers; D76-D77(bg), Andy Caulfield/The Image Bank; D78, James H. Carmichael, Jr./The Image Bank.

Unit E, Harcourt Brace & Company Photographs: E4-E5, Weronica Ankarorn; E6(t), Earl Kogler; E6(b), Dick Krueger; E8, E9, Weronica Ankarorn; E10-E11, E13, E14(t), E14(b), E15, Earl Kogler; E16, Weronica Ankarorn; E17, E20, E23, E24, E27, E29, E30, E38(t), E41(t), E41(b), E50, E57, E61, Earl Kogler; E91(r), Dick Krueger; E92(t), Earl Kogler; E92(b), Maria Paraskevas; E93, Dick Krueger.

Unit E, All Other Photographs: Unit Page Divider, Frank P. Rossotto/The Stock Market; E1, E2-E3, Neena M. Wilmot/ Stock/Art Images; E2, Archiv/Photo Researchers; E3, Frank P. Rossotto/The Stock Market; E7, Milt & Joan Mann/Camera-mann; E12(bg), Craig Aurness/West Light; E12(t), Allen S. Stone/Devaney Stock Photos; E12(b), Kennon Cooke/Valan Photos; E21, Wide World Photos; E26(bg), M. Stephenson/West Light; E26(t), K. Sklute/SuperStock; E26(b) North Wind; E30-E31(bg), Alese & Mort Pechter/The Stock Market; E33, Ron Watts/Black Star; E35, Linc Cornell/Light Sources; E38(bg), J.A. Kraulis/Masterfile; E38(b), Norman Owen Tomalin/Bruce Coleman, Inc.; E40(t), Russ Kinne/Comstock; E40(b), Spencer Swanger/Tom Stack & Assoc.; E47, William Carter/Photo Researchers; E54(bg), Paul Chesley/Tony Stone Images; E54(t), Steve Kaufman/Ken Graham Agency; E54(b), UPI/Bettmann; E55(tl), Percy Jones/Archive Photos; E55(tr), Photri; E55(c), Charles Palek/Tom Stack & Assoc.; E55(bl), Photri; E55(br), Frank P. Rossotto/Tom Stack & Assoc.; E60(l), Richard P. Smith/Tom Stack & Assoc.; E60(r), Ken Gouvin/Comstock; E62, Gerald & Buff Corsi/Tom Stack & Assoc.; E63(t), Gary Benson/ Comstock; E63(b), John McDermott/Tony Stone Images; E64(t), Neena M. Wilmot/Stock/Art Images; E64(b), John Shaw/Tom Stack & Assoc.; E65, Bruce Matheson/PHOTO/NATS; E66, Archive Photos; E67, UPI/Bettmann Newsphotos; E68, The Bettmann Archive; E70, E71, U.S. Air Force; E72(bg), NASA; E72(t), NASA/Photri; E72(b), E78, NASA; E79, J. Novak/SuperStock; E80(t), Hank Brandli and Rob Downey; E80(b), European Space Agency/Photo Researchers; E81, David R. Frazier; E82, NASA/Photri; E84, E86(t), E86(c), NASA; E86(b), E87(t), Frank P. Rossotto/Tom Stack & Assoc.; E87(c), NASA; E87(b), W. Kaufmann/Photo Researchers; E88(tl), NASA; E88(tr), E88(c), E88(bl), E88(br), NASA/Photri; E89(t), NASA; E89(b), NASA/Photri; E90-E91(bg), Wendy Shattil, Bob Rozinski/Tom Stack & Assoc.; E91(l), NASA; E92-E93(bg), Greg Vaughn/Tom Stack & Assoc.; E94, Gerald & Buff Corsi/Tom Stack & Assoc.; E95, NASA.